AD

Architectural Design
May/June 2009

Energies
New Material Boundaries
Guest-edited by Sean Lally

D1202564

IN THIS ISSUE
Main Section

WILEY
wiley.com

Architectural Design

Vol 79 No 3
May/June 2009
ISBN 978-0470 753637

Editorial Offices
John Wiley & Sons
International House
Ealing Broadway Centre
London W5 5DB

T: +44 (0)20 8326 3800

Editor
Helen Castle

Regular columnists: Valentina Croci, David Littlefield, Jayne Merkel, Will McLean, Neil Spiller, Michael Weinstock and Ken Yeang

Freelance Managing Editor
Caroline Ellerby

Production Editor
Elizabeth Gongde

Design and Prepress
Artmedia, London

Printed in Italy by Conti Tipocolor

Sponsorship/advertising
Faith Pidduck/Wayne Frost
T: +44 (0)1243 770254
E: fpidduck@wiley.co.uk

Front cover: WEATHERS, Amplification installation, Part of the Gen(h)ome Project, Schindler House, MAK Center for Art and Architecture, Los Angeles, 2006–07. Image courtesy of the MAK Center, photo Joshua White.

Subscribe to △D

△D is published bimonthly and is available to purchase on both a subscription basis and as individual volumes at the following prices.

PRICES
Individual copies: £22.99/$45.00
Mailing fees may apply

ANNUAL SUBSCRIPTION RATES
Student: UK£70/US$110 print only
Individual: UK £110/US$170 print only
Institutional: UK£180/US$335 print or online
Institutional: UK£198/US$369 combined print and online

Subscription Offices UK
John Wiley & Sons Ltd
Journals Administration Department
1 Oldlands Way, Bognor Regis
West Sussex, PO22 9SA
T: +44 (0)1243 843272
F: +44 (0)1243 843232
E: cs-journals@wiley.co.uk

[ISSN: 0003-8504]

Prices are for six issues and include postage and handling charges. Periodicals postage paid at Jamaica, NY 11431. Air freight and mailing in the USA by Publications Expediting Services Inc, 200 Meacham Avenue, Elmont, NY 11003.
Individual rate subscriptions must be paid by personal cheque or credit card. Individual rate subscriptions may not be resold or used as library copies.

All prices are subject to change without notice.

Postmaster
Send address changes to 3 Publications Expediting Services, 200 Meacham Avenue, Elmont, NY 11003

RIGHTS AND PERMISSIONS
Requests to the Publisher should be addressed to:
Permissions Department
John Wiley & Sons Ltd
The Atrium
Southern Gate
Chichester
West Sussex PO19 8SQ
England

F: +44 (0)1243 770620
E: permreq@wiley.co.uk

C O N T E N T S

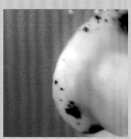

Editorial

Helen Castle

In this title of *AD*, guest-editor Sean Lally challenges our preconceptions of what architecture might be. He removes the walls from around us and the very roof from above our heads by questioning the established boundaries of architectural structure. He asks us to suspend our belief in the concrete matter of building as the foundation of architecture, whether it is the physical qualities of glass and steel or the Modernist notion of space, light and volume. Instead, he requires us to focus on the invisible rather than the visible: on material energies as the generative driver of design. Static materiality is replaced by the dynamics of thermodynamic exchange. The energy model or fluid dynamic diagram usurps the place of structure or outer shell; the impact is not unlike that of a Victorian seeing an X-ray for the first time and experiencing the revelation of looking beyond the exoskeleton.

For both Lally (see his Gradient Spatial Typologies project, p 9) and Philippe Rahm (Research House for Dominique Gonzalez-Foerster, p 38), material energies become the *raison d'être* for social and spatial organisation of domestic space. Temperature and climate might determine layout or the use of rooms, as the occupants are encouraged to migrate seasonally from one space to another. For Cristina Díaz Moreno and Efrén García Grinda of AMID (Cero9) energy becomes the inspiration and the fuel for a new formal language and spatial understanding (see pp 76–83). The relationship with energies does not have to be so immediate. In experiments with biological form, the energy of the sun becomes the main life-giving force (see pp 48–53).

This focus on energies requires a watershed in thinking. It is by necessity a process of inversion of accepted architectural design practices, requiring a new manner of conceiving space and its organisation. The term 'energies' all too easily strikes up associations with energy-efficient architecture. Lally and his contributors are wary of this connotation and of its being mistaken as a further mutation of green architecture. In her article, Penelope Dean explicitly distances the approach from the well-trodden track of sustainability, as one that is too embedded in matter and the gizmos of environmental techno-science (pp 24–9). The quest is for a new conceptual model for architecture. At only a nascent stage in its investigations, *Energies* requires a leap into the dark, but it also proves wonderfully revitalising in its explorations as it requires us to look at generative design afresh. ∆

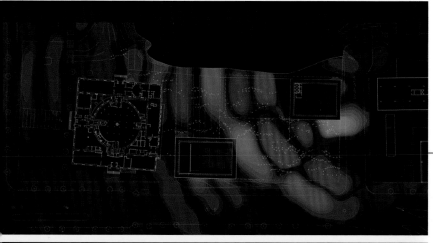

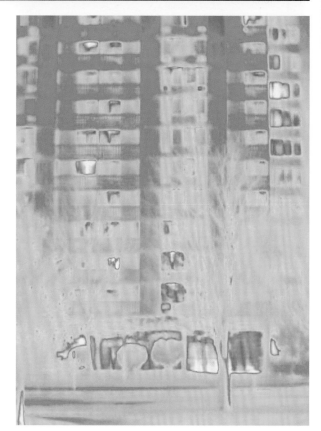

WEATHERS, Asplund Library Competition, Stockholm, 2006
The proposed library addition operates beyond the envelope of a building or site boundary and engages the surrounding environmental qualities and seasonal climatic conditions for programmatic and organisational strategies.

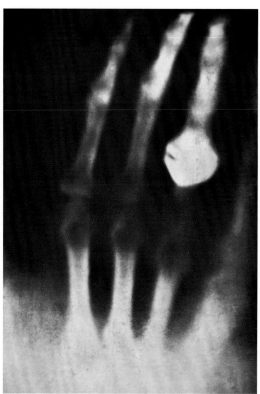

Wilhelm Röntgen, *Hand mit Ringen* (Hand with Rings), 1895
This first 'medical' X-ray taken by Röntgen of his wife's hand. Seeing this view inside the human body for the first time must have been a revelation.

A thermogram of an apartment building
This thermogram highlights which apartments have their heat turned up, and which have their windows open; the temperature ranges from hot (white) to cold (blue). Generally used to express heat radiation in built or designed projects, the *Energies* approach enables us to consider the possibilities of thermodynamics for generative design.

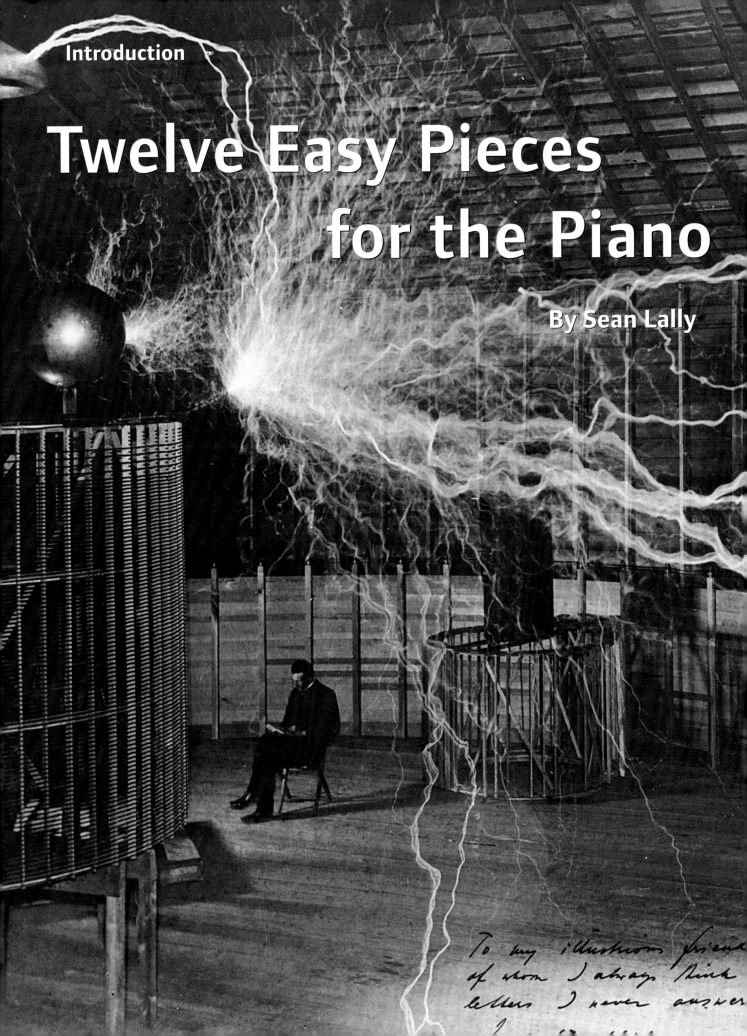

Twelve Easy Pieces
for the Piano

By Sean Lally

To my illustrious friend
of whom I always think
letters I never answer

Inventor and mechanical and electrical engineer Nikola Tesla (1856–1943) in his Colorado Springs laboratory as 18-metre (60-foot) electrical sparks leap across the room. Tesla believed that energy exists in the strata of ether that constantly surrounds us, to be tapped and harnessed as we see fit.

The work presented in this issue is intended to instigate a discussion regarding the spectrum of materiality found in and around the structures, or geometries and forms, that designers traditionally rely on to define a physical boundary. These 'material energies' of thermal variation, air velocity, light spectra and electricity all have potential roles beyond merely producing moods or effects along a surface. Yet this potential is often explored through little more than metaphors and poetics; worse, it is seen only as a resource for creating preconceived, rule-of-thumb interior comfort zones and energy-efficient buildings. The issue looks to ways of releasing these material energies from their dependence on surfaces and services to deploy them as building materials in and of themselves: redefining the physical boundaries and edges that architects use as organisation strategies opens the potential for design innovation and the creation of new spatial and social constructs.

A crucial component of the architectural profession has been its ability to appropriate the tools, techniques and research of adjacent disciplines while simultaneously stretching the limits of what is possible in the design and construction of our built environment. Yet when it comes to energy – one of the most prevalent and ubiquitous materials to influence architecture and its related disciplines in the last 30 years – only stunted attempts have been made to explore its design possibilities. Two mutually exclusive mantras have been adopted: 'sustainability', which has kept us locked in discussions of efficiency and preconceived notions of individual comfort levels (interior heating and cooling), and 'atmosphere', which proposes using these same materialities to convey an ambient quality. Instead we must engage these material energies as something generative or explorative: to appropriate, mutate and bastardise temperature gradients, air masses, luminosity, plant physiology, scent and humidity indexes. How can these materialities take on more responsibility in architectural designs, acting as physical boundaries and organisational systems?

As designers of our built environment, whether architects, landscape architects or urban planners we essentially dictate instructions for constructing the boundaries between things. As architects we organise and delineate activities, constructing boundaries to permit and foster their operation. Methods for defining and separating activities, including devising the necessary thresholds for their connection, and the resultant hierarchies dictated by this organisation of activities are forged and fortified by the boundaries we construct. The methods of circulation that guide our movement, the nodes we use to congregate and gather, and even the mullion-free glass curtain wall that connects us to a million-dollar beachfront view are all formed by the boundaries constructed between a range of unmediated materiality on one (outer) side and the comfort-controlled versions of those very same materialities on the other (inner) side. Whether or not we are immediately conscious of it, the boundaries that we design and construct today are developed within a rather narrow bandwidth of available materiality, which for the most part results in a solid-state construction. This issue of *AD* broadens that bandwidth of available materiality for constructing such physical boundaries.

Material Energies

If we are to rely less on surfaces and geometries as material boundaries, what then are our options? What other material boundary can architects operate on during the design phase and the construction of a building? Physicists define a boundary not as a tangible thing, but rather as an action, seeing the environment as an energy field where boundaries are transitional states of that field.[1] Boundaries are

The materiality that exists beyond the 'walls' of architecture is clearly no longer outside human action. The question is, will we begin to act upon it directly, engaging it as a materiality and design opportunity, or will it act on us only indirectly as a second- and third-hand repercussion? Left: Mathieu Lehanneur, O from Elements project, 2006, finessing variable levels of oxygen in our domestic spaces. Top right: Pasona O, Tokyo, Japan, 2007, controlling spectrums of light (red versus blue) that stimulate either vegetative green growth or flower blooms. Bottom right: Zbigniew Oksiuta and VG Bild-Kunst Bonn, Biological Forms in Space, 2005.

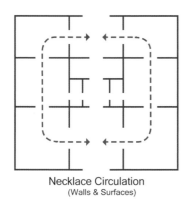

Necklace Circulation
(Walls & Surfaces)

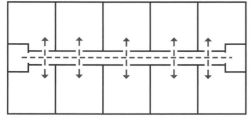

Corridors and Destinations
(Walls & Surfaces)

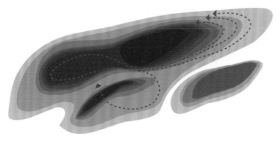

Gradients of Intensities
(Material Energies)

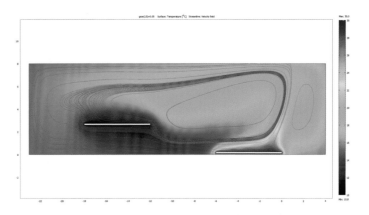

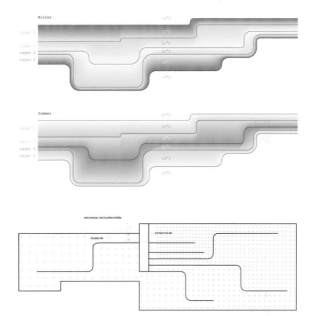

Sean Lally, Gradient Spatial Typologies Diagram, 2008
In his article 'Figures, doors and passages', Robin Evans reminds us that strategies we use to divide space simultaneously play a role in how we as inhabitants are brought back together, and points to the implications this has on our spatial and social organisations. Gradient Spatial Typologies is a look at how these material energies can offer opportunities for future organisation.

Philippe Rahm Architects, Digestible Gulf Stream, Venice Biennale (2008), Tadeusz Kantor Museum, Poland (2006) and the AIRGRAPHIA sport pavilion, Rhône-Saône development (2008)
Reinvestigating the plan cut allows for a fundamental re-evaluation of architectural language and principles, as well as providing a necessary platform from which to periodically rearticulate its implications as we look to material energies and the spatial typologies they create and provide.

understood as behaviours that remain variable and exist only when energy is transitioning from one state to another. Climate engineers and meteorologists as well as mechanical engineers have techniques for visualising gradient conditions of atmospheric pressure as well as thermal boundaries and air velocity. The characteristics of these material energies, once the focus is shifted from surfaces and geometries as primary methods of delineating boundary edges, become the behaviours of these edges, which act more as gradients of intensities, feathering and overlapping each other as they interact. Such materialities – the shifting intensity and variability of spectra of light, thermal diffusions and transfers, levels of relative humidity, and even our range of olfactory

sensitivity – come into existence when we can act upon them and give them organisational responsibilities. They offer an opportunity to understand boundaries not as static lines or surfaces, but as fluctuating intensities read best as a gradient condition.

More than Auras
One of the underlying threads of this issue is to address how material energies can become the physical boundaries that construct architecture. To achieve this, architects must acknowledge that so far they have stunted the growth and potentiality of material energies by curtailing the responsibility placed upon them. Using terms such as 'atmosphere', 'effect' or 'sensation' to explore and define conditions of interest affords few physical means or notions as to how to quantify, measure and control them. They are terminologies of intention without

a clear directive for implementation or, more importantly, for assessing implications. The means of control are hidden within, layered beneath and simultaneously acknowledged and overlooked in these material energies, and as a result they are relegated to something closer to a desired by-product. Defining them as atmospheric qualities implies a minimal amount of responsibility: they do not prevent rain from falling on our heads, they do not provide privacy or control crowds of people, and they do not push back strongly enough against the activities and events that exist around them to inform and control the subsequent spatial organisation, either intentionally or subversively. They are simply cosmetic.[2]

These effects, atmospheres and sensations rely on the constructed surface to produce them. Architects strive for little more than to produce a quality in a predefined space, a sensation in an already defined geometric boundary, or an effect using a material that already constructs the boundaries of the space. This only hints at the potential of material energies, which appear as ancestral forms of what today should be assuming an additional level of responsibility and directly engaging the organisational structure of the activities on hand. As yet these are not materials per se, but seductive by-products that divert our attention from what is doing the real work, what is actually controlling the spatial and organisational strategies of the spaces we define and create: the surface. This publication does not call for the elimination of such effects and qualities, but it does definitively state that there must be something more at stake: as the profession seeks design innovation, the surface must no longer act as the sole initiator.

Surface Comfort

The surface plays a decisive role in tempering architectural spaces, selecting what passes through to, or is prevented from accessing, the spaces beyond (breezes, light, etc): the surface is the sole mediation device. And when the surface is not mediating exterior climatic contexts, it acts as a hermetically sealed membrane around internally generated climates, operating in collusion with industry standards to maintain and provide common notions of comfort zones, sealing within the energies that produce these homogeneous interiors. When it comes to nearly all issues associated with environmental design, the all-too-well-referenced Reyner Banham is never far behind. In his book *The Architecture of the Well-Tempered Environment* (1969)[3] he discusses three methods for dealing with and subverting existing climatic conditions to meet these comfort needs, all of which privilege the surface above all else. The 'conservative' approach requires a wall and its materials

WEATHERS, Amplification installation, part of the Gen(h)ome Project, Schindler House, MAK Center for Art and Architecture, Los Angeles, 2006-07
Simulations in COSMOS (a fluid dynamic modelling software often deployed in mechanical engineering) permit a visualisation of materials, including thermal transfers and air velocities. In the Amplification project, these materialities, as well as vegetation, light and scent, are controlled and amplified through the discrete triggers of artificial heating devices, fans, lighting and fluorescent dyes in an attempt to produce microclimates of heat, water vapour, condensation and air particulates unique to each of the six units on the site.

(much like adobe structures) to provide a thermal lag that limits heat during the day yet radiates that collected heat at night to warm interiors; the 'selective' method entails tuning exterior walls, roofs and floors to filter existing breezes and provide shade from the sun, all in an attempt to mediate existing conditions within the interior; and the 'generative' method relies on the sealing and closing of these surface conditions to allow artificial heating and cooling systems to provide the desired interior comfort.

Each of these methods places the surface at the foreground, with the potential exception of the generative approach, where heating and cooling equipment is primary. However, even in this case the surface is the demarcation line of what stays in and what gets out. As we have come to see in the advancements made in curtain-wall construction, the surface that wraps these spaces and interiors has not only grown to enhance many of these conservative, selective or generative aspects, but has also seen to it that all spatial organisations and boundaries are coincident with the surface. Material energies, for the most part, are either reflected, selected or internally created, taking on a rather minimal amount of responsibility themselves. Little is asked from them other than to supply a rather subjective level of comfort to our bodies. Thus they have been relegated to conditioning predefined interiors or to acting as special effects in creating moods or atmospheres. In either case, the surface has been doing the heavy lifting, and material energies have simply played a supporting role. The work featured in this issue is in pursuit of alternatives to this relationship. The intention is not simply to break down borders between inside and outside in an attempt to overcome the excessively

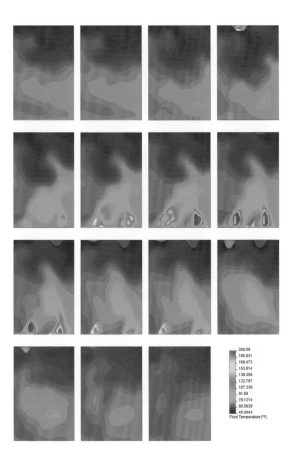

Peter Lang, Liquid Levitation Sculptures
(Ferrofluid, Neodym, Microcontroller), 2007
Whether physically visible or not, materials
including a magnetic force can influence the
physical spaces we define and inhabit.

engineered line that demarcates the interior/exterior divide, but rather to see if we can do away with the line altogether.

The articles here provide an introduction to a discussion that is gaining traction and momentum well beyond what exists between these covers. The issue draws from the work of architects, artists and writers who seek a similar conversation, which is amplified as they are juxtaposed against one another. The contributions range in scope from the historical contextualisation of the mechanical delivery systems that architects rarely question yet dutifully incorporate within their architecture today, to design competitions and commissions that focus more on the organisational implications than the available technologies. The issue also includes installations that seek to further illustrate these intentions, as well as the work of designers who operate within a realm that is closer to that of a biologist – not merely by mimicking structural forces and geometry, but rather by augmenting and mutating the chemical process (the photosynthesis of colour, pigment, scent) to produce systems of inhabitation. Such projects look to the spatial typologies that emerge from the biases and proclivities of material energies, the types and scales of the physical boundaries they make and the related circulation strategies, as well as the shortcomings and strengths that arise – some of which may not always be immediately recognisable, subversively occurring like undercurrents that take iterations to bring to the foreground.

Most importantly, though, the overarching focus and intent of the issue is to examine the potential repercussions of such research and design strategies. If material energies are moved to the foreground, are given the same responsibility as materialities that construct physical boundaries and allowed to create various new spatial typologies, what might be the spatial and social implications to our built surroundings? Robin Evans (1944–93) reminds us that the strategies used to divide space simultaneously play a role in how we as inhabitants are brought back together, and points out the implications of this for our social organisation.[4] The projects and texts featured here strive to project opportunities rather than provide solutions in the strategies they deploy. This is an important distinction, as it sets the architect and designer, rather than the environmental engineer, at the helm of these investigations. It is thus necessary for architects and designers to stretch their imaginations and cut that which tethers them to preconceived notions. ⟁

Notes

1. D Michelle Addington and Daniel L Schodek, *Smart Materials and New Technologies: For the Architecture and Design Professions*, Architectural Press (London), 2004, p 7.
2. Jeffrey Kipnis, 'The Cunning of Cosmetics', *El Croquis 60 + 84 Herzog and DeMeuron 1981–2000*, El Croquis (Madrid), 1997, pp 26.
3. Reyner Banham, *The Architecture of the Well-Tempered Environment*, University of Chicago Press (Chicago, IL), 1969, p 23.
4. Robin Evans, 'Figures, doors and passages', *Translations From Drawing to Building and Other Essays*, MIT Press (Cambridge, MA), 1997, p 56.

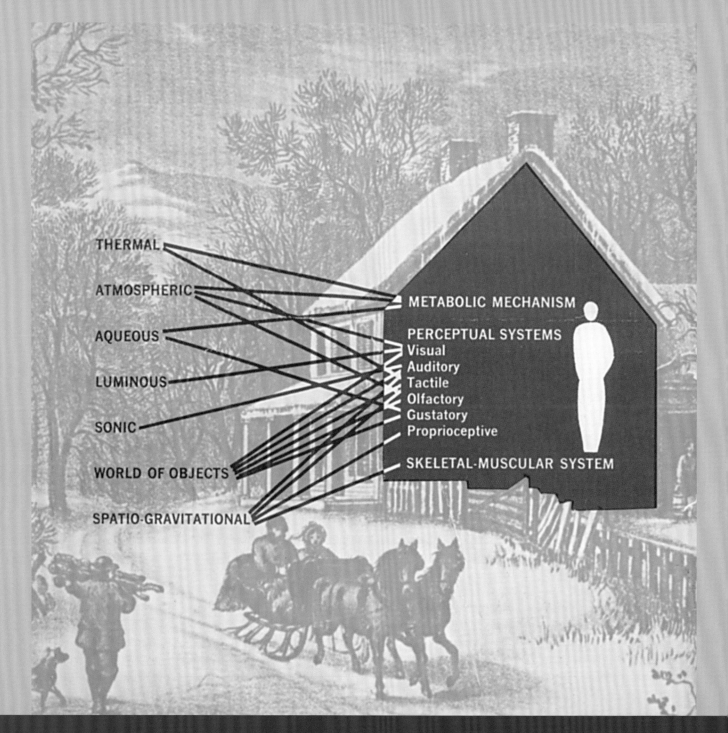

Contingent Behaviours

Michelle Addington questions the accepted Modernist conception of the interior as a hermetically sealed envelope. She highlights the vicissitudes in attitudes that have existed over time to interior and exterior conditions by flagging up the 19th-century pursuit of ventilation and the permeable outside wall, which was pursued in the quest for public sanitation and a misguided belief in the 'toxic' interior.

Architectural critic and historian James Marston Fitch, in his influential work *American Building 2: The Environmental Forces That Shape It* (1972), stated that 'the ultimate task of architecture is to act in favor of man: to interpose itself between man and the natural environment in which he finds himself, in such a way as to remove the gross environmental load from his shoulders.'[1] This description is certainly not profound; indeed it seems quite prosaic as the attribute of shelter has been considered as both the fundamental essence and the ultimate purpose of architecture for millennia.

Fitch's seminal image of man encased in an environment wholly contained within the building envelope serves as the accepted manifestation of architecture as well as the ultimate determinant of man's animate perceptions and wellbeing.

Fitch's seminal image of man encased in an environment wholly contained within the building envelope serves as the accepted manifestation of architecture as well as the ultimate determinant of man's animate perceptions and wellbeing. The building as shelter was never saddled with the need to provide for comfort, as it served only to ameliorate those extreme conditions that were beyond the human body's ability for adaptation. The exterior walls of a building were mediating elements, negotiating between the needs of the body and the extant environment. These elements of environmental mediation were embedded in the vernacular, determining form and materials more directly and persistently than local or regional culture. Buildings in low-pressure primary climates had similar roof slopes and solid-to-void ratios regardless of whether they were located in Bangkok or New Orleans, and buildings in high-pressure climates had similar thermal-mass materials and surface-to-volume ratios regardless of whether they were located in Mozambique or Arizona. The laws of heat transfer – conduction, convection, radiation – were made manifest through the boundary of the building. Although the term 'boundary' often connotes the physical extent of a building – its envelope – in the realm of heat transfer,

the boundary is the zone within which energy exchanges take place. These fundamental energy exchanges are explicitly denoted in Fitch's image as residing in the envelope, and as such 'envelope' becomes coincident with 'boundary' which then becomes implicitly coincident with 'mediation.' In this image, the human body is but a passive component, an ancillary element whose energy exchanges are wholly determined by the superposed active envelope.

This subordination of body to building reflects a different characterisation of the envelope, one in which it functions as a 'container' of the environment of man and a 'barrier' to the environment of nature. This second and perhaps more intractable characterisation is an altogether different concept than that of environmental mediation and one that did not arise until the advent of environmental technologies for conditioning the interior. The development of environmental technologies, particularly HVAC (heating, ventilation and air conditioning) during the late 19th and early 20th centuries is widely credited with introducing comfort while simultaneously freeing the building from its role as environmental mediator. The sleek glass facades that were the iconic representation of Modernism were possible only because the building siting and materials could be decoupled from the interior environment. The mechanical and electrical systems that provided heat, light and air or removed excess heat, humidity and odours were comprised of discrete components that had no requisite relationship to the building structure.

Released from the obligation to mediate between the exterior and interior, 20th-century architecture presented unprecedented opportunities to explore new materials and to experiment with form. Early 20th-century architects, including Le Corbusier and Frank Lloyd Wright, interpreted this environmental decoupling of the envelope as its transformation from a boundary of exchange to a boundary of discontinuity, even using the term 'hermetic' to describe the envelope's new role.[2] Nevertheless, the concept of isolating interior from exterior was only implicit, and it did not become explicit and operational until the field of architecture theorised the interior environment as a disconnected other. The use of environmental technologies set the stage for the substitution of the interior environment with an altered and reconfigured environment that was distinguished from the exterior by its level of conditioning. The more it was conditioned, the more independent it became from exterior conditions. It became a manufactured rather than a mediated environment. Ironically, however, by supplanting survival with comfort, the environmental technologies ultimately increased the dependence of the building design on form and materials, particularly those of its 'envelope'. The envelope has morphed from its role as the mediator of surrounding conditions to the determinant of those conditions.

The isolated and contained interior environment may seem to be the optimum utilisation of HVAC technology, yet it represents an abrupt switch from the origins of environmental technologies. Indeed, the early 20th-century HVAC system emerged from a desire to increase the

James Marston Fitch's classic image of the building envelope mediating between the environments of man and nature. From *American Building 2: The Environmental Forces That Shape It* (1972).

connection between interior and exterior in the 19th century. At the beginning of the 19th century, the fear of exterior miasmas began to shift into a concern about 'toxic' interior conditions. Increased overcrowding in urban areas, coupled with the knowledge gleaned from the developing science of air chemistry, led to a widely accepted theory regarding the human contamination of air. Body odour was presumed to result from 'putrefaction', or rotting skin, and the carbon dioxide exhaled in each breath was considered to be highly poisonous.[3] Ventilation with outside air of any quality was seen as the only solution to preventing the spread of illness and death. Openings were added to building facades to encourage cross-ventilation, and large chases pierced multiple floors to exploit density-driven ventilation.

By the end of the 19th century, the impetus for 'fresh' outdoor air further accelerated the desire for ventilation as it was widely believed to be a prophylactic measure against tuberculosis. As the rates of tuberculosis increased, buildings were opened even further, culminating in the open-air movement in which walls began to disappear as the boundary between inside and outside was erased.[4] Unfortunately, ventilation offered no such protection against epidemics, and the 1918 flu epidemic resurrected old fears about disease-laden miasmas wafting in from the exterior. Building openings were abruptly sealed and fledgling HVAC manufacturers were quick to capitalise on this – advertising their systems as producing manufactured environments that were 'cleaner and purer than what nature could provide'.[5]

The 19th-century origin of ventilation had resulted in an increasingly permeable building with a more immediate connection to the exterior whereas the 20th-century application of HVAC systems resulted in an impermeable envelope that isolated the interior. Corollary to this overprivileging of the building envelope as a barrier to the exterior is the configuration of the interior as a homogeneous, ideal environment. Environmental determinists such as Ellsworth Huntington were equating cooler environmental temperatures with the superior races, and the medical establishment was clinging to the belief that diseases from tuberculosis to cancer were exacerbated in warm conditions.[6] The quest for the 'perfect' temperature gathered steam and all but eclipsed research into the physiological interaction of the body with transient thermal behaviours. Empirical studies trumped analytical research as the irrationality of a perfect environment precluded the application of the laws of physics. Numerous studies were conducted during which occupants were polled as to the conditions they found to be satisfactory. A measure known as the Predicted Mean Vote (PMV) collapsed together a large array of data so as

to help define the environmental conditions that would likely receive the most neutral (as opposed to too warm or too cool) votes and the American Society of Heating, Refrigerating and Air-Conditioning Engineers (ASHRAE) developed the prevailing definition of thermal comfort as 'those conditions in which 80% of the occupants do not express discomfort'.[7] Essentially, the goal for designing the interior environment became the delivery of conditions that one would not notice.

Until the 1970s, the homogeneous interior environment lived up to its one criterion – it was not noticed. There was so much thermal inertia in the large volumes of air circulating inside the building that the body was subordinated to its surroundings: the interior environment drove the body's heat exchange rather than the reverse. Given that there were relatively constant levels of activity, for example office workers stayed seated for most of the day, this immersion in steady-state conditions was effective even if not efficient. The oil embargo of 1973 resulted in an almost overnight switch in HVAC

The performative envelope is known by many terms – polyvalent wall, intelligent facade, high-performance envelope, smart skin, double-skin wall – that essentially refer to a thickened envelope housing many mechanical and electrical functions, of which the most elaborate constructions are highly engineered, from photosensors to 'smart' glazings.

control strategies away from large volumes at constant delivery rates to smaller volumes at variable rates.[8] The thermal inertia that was the fundamental premise behind the operation of the HVAC system was sacrificed for lower energy costs. As the inertia was reduced, issues with comfort and health increased as the new variability in the interior environment had little to do with the thermal exchange of any individual occupant. The building envelope loomed as a major player as its thermal conditions became the driving force. Any perturbation in the thermal environment – from a human body standing up after being seated, to a cloud suddenly obscuring the solar radiation entering through a glazed surface – would set off a Rube Goldberg chain of reactions of which the final result was a change in airflow rates to a zone. While the response could be considered to be local, as zones can be as small as a room, the locality relates to the assignation of bounded spaces. Each space, then, is still seen as a contained environment with the same criterion of neutrality and with the body being treated as a generalisable yet problematic input.

Much of the attention now being paid to environmental systems stems from a desire to return to the steady conditions produced by

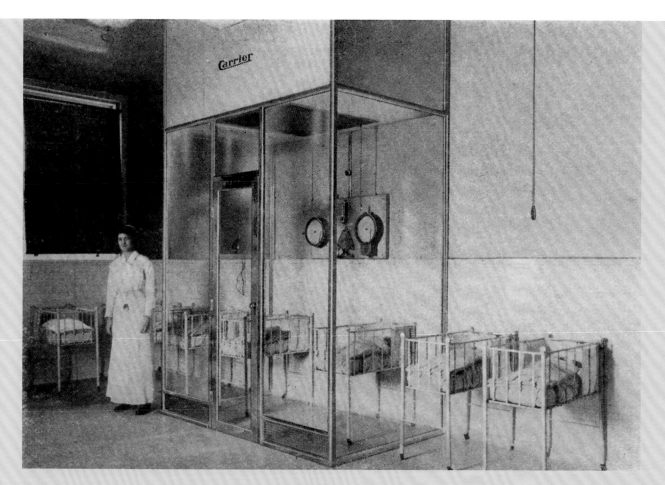

In this 1919 advertisement for the Carrier Engineering Corporation, a hospital incubator is pictured with the caption: 'Even babies can be manufactured with manufactured weather.' From *The Story of Manufactured Weather* (1919).

high-inertia systems but delivered by the more variable and less expensive low-inertia systems. The inability of the contemporary HVAC system to maintain neutrality is often blamed on inadequate control systems or on poorly designed envelopes. Indeed, the variability of the conditions in the interior is more likely than not greater than those of the exterior. 'High-performance' buildings emerged as a typological solution to this variability, with much of their focus placed on the technological enhancement of the building envelope. Designed to absorb many of the functions of the HVAC system, the performative envelope became the signature element of the type. The ever-increasing compression of functionality into the envelope gave rise to the misconception that it mediates between exterior and interior conditions and, as such, to the presumption that it is the contemporary manifestation of the mediating boundary.

The performative envelope is known by many terms – polyvalent wall, intelligent facade, high-performance envelope, smart skin, double-skin wall – that essentially refer to a thickened envelope housing many mechanical and electrical functions, of which the most elaborate constructions are highly engineered, from photosensors to 'smart' glazings. It certainly seems as though this is a return to the idea of the envelope as an environmental mediator. Adjustable louvres control the amount of sunlight entering the building, secondary fans directly exhaust the solar energy absorbed on the facade before it enters the building, and multiple layers of glass provide wind and noise management. The performative envelope is the ultimate manifestation of Fitch's image, but with a tautological twist: most of the embedded technologies are necessary only because of the prima facie decision to have a fully glazed facade. Rather than mediating between interior and exterior, the performative wall is compensating for the environmental penalties wrought by a material choice. If the advent of HVAC enabled the application of the

Modernist glazed facade, then the contemporary glazed facade demands additional technologies and systems so that the HVAC systems conditioning the interior environment can function adequately.

The concept of the determinant envelope has been a difficult one to dislodge. Over the course of the 20th century, the science of heat transfer and fluid mechanics underwent a radical reformation, the field of neurobiology began to identify and analyse the human body's complex interactions with its thermal and luminous environment, and the discipline of engineering developed a vast array of unprecedented materials and technologies. None of these advances have led to a reconfiguration of the purpose and function of the building envelope. Nor has the growth in building-related illnesses, of which most are attributed to overly sealed buildings and poorly functioning HVAC systems, spawned any reconsideration. Indeed, more than a century later the prevailing mantra of building construction is 'Build Tight, Ventilate Right'.[9] Essentially, the belief in the concept of the sealed environment is so pervasive that any problems with it are attributed to a lack of commitment to its rigorous application.

Noticeably missing from the discourse on environmental systems is any challenge to the concept of the building as container of the body's environment. The understanding of the thermal exchange between a human body and its surroundings is much different at the beginning of the 21st century than it was in the 20th century. The body's heat exchange with its interior surroundings primarily takes place in two ways. The first is through convective exchange between the skin's surface and its buoyant boundary layer. The conditions of air beyond the few centimetres thickness of the layer are relevant only insofar as they impact buoyant movement. Many of the thermal management technologies that are ubiquitous in electronics cooling are more than capable of locally controlling that movement, rendering obsolete the need to do so via the indirect and inefficient means of large, homogeneously conditioned volumes of air. The second primary mode is radiant exchange between the body's skin and the surrounding heat sources and sinks. The body is always negotiating with a transient field of sources and sinks; the thoughtful location of just a few could readily maintain thermoregulatory function regardless of the air temperature. Furthermore, the thermoregulatory system responds to different inputs than does the thermal sensory system and both can be manipulated by local and discrete changes, enabling one to decouple the interactions.

The necessary thermal exchanges for maintaining the health of the body have much larger tolerances than those that determine sensation, and are also located in different regions of the body. The blood flow to the forehead, neck and core drives insensate thermoregulation, the body's peripheral receptors determine cognitive sensation. A rigorous application of current knowledge regarding local heat transfer coupled with existing technologies could easily manage the thermal needs and sensations of each and every body, and do so with orders of magnitude less energy use; yet the field of architecture will not relinquish its hegemonic privileging of the building as the primary determining factor. If today's overly complex envelope can be seen as an extrapolation of Fitch's mediating wall, then we should also note that Fitch's version is but a rhetorical image of architecture as the centre of the physical world. In this image, the building envelope serves as a boundary that is simultaneously an extension of the body and an intension of the surrounding environment.

Even though developments in analysing and simulating the interior environment have revealed the remarkable variability and transiency of that environment, we stubbornly cling to the belief that the envelope supersedes all – acting as a barrier to the exterior, container of the interior and determinant of all extant physical phenomena. Essentially, we privilege that which we know, that which we see, that which matches our image of a permanent and static architecture.

Even though developments in analysing and simulating the interior environment have revealed the remarkable variability and transiency of that environment, we stubbornly cling to the belief that the envelope supersedes all – acting as a barrier to the exterior, container of the interior and determinant of all extant physical phenomena. Essentially, we privilege that which we know, that which we see, that which matches our image of a permanent and static architecture. In *The Architecture of the Well-Tempered Environment*, Reyner Banham wrote that those 'cultures whose members organize their environment by means of massive structures tend to visualize space as they have lived in it, that is bounded and contained, limited by walls, floors and ceilings'.[10] Banham was here differentiating the universally modern from the vernacular in which the former's use of glazing enabled visual spaces extending beyond the planes of the building's surfaces. This may be so, but the modern remains resolutely wedded to conceptualising the human environment as bounded and contained. △

During the open-air school movement, classrooms were progressively opened up to the exterior environment even during the winter. From *Open Air Crusaders* (1913).

Notes

1. James Marston Fitch, *American Building 2: The Environmental Forces That Shape It*, Houghton-Mifflin (Boston, MA), 1972, p 1.

2. During a lecture given in Brazil in 1929, Le Corbusier drew a sketch that represented a multifloor building as a singular entity, completely sealed from the exterior environment by a continuous, impenetrable envelope, and conditioned as a homogeneous volume with an air handler fully responsible for managing the interior. He annotated his sketch with *bâtiments hermitiques* while exclaiming 'The house is sealed fast!'. (See *Precisions on the Present State of Architecture and City Planning*, trans E Aujame, MIT Press (Cambridge, MA), 1991, pp 64–6). The expression 'hermetic' was also used by Frank Lloyd Wright in his autobiography when he described the Larkin Building as 'a simple cliff of brick hermetically sealed to keep the interior space clear of the poisonous gases…'. (See *An Autobiography*, Horizon Press (New York), 1977, p 175.

3. After Lavoisier and others identified the chemical components of air in the late 18th century, there was a progressive interest in carbonic acid, which is essentially carbon dioxide combined with water. Studies of animals in sealed environments led to the conclusion that their demise was due to an increase in carbonic acid rather than a decrease in oxygen.

4. The open-air movement grew out of the popular outdoor cure that placed tubercular patients in Alpine-like settings. In dense urban areas, particularly those crowded with tenements, few patients were able to partake of a visit to a sanatorium, so residents were encouraged to sleep on roofs, on fire escapes, or anywhere that might take them outside. Open-air schools emerged as a way to provide 'fresh' air to children from the tenements, and were eventually expanded so that schoolchildren from Boston to Chicago were taught in classrooms that had open windows even in the middle of winter. An excellent archival source on the movement is Sherman Kingsley, *Open Air Crusaders*, The Elizabeth McCormick Memorial Fund (Chicago, IL), 1913.

5. See Carrier Engineering Corporation, *The Story of Manufactured Weather*, Carrier Engineering Corporation (New York), 1919, p 5.

6. Ellsworth Huntington argued that 'climate alone among the great inanimate features of the human environment produces direct physiological effects'. Huntington described the ideal climate as being one quite similar to New England where he not so coincidentally was teaching. See Ellsworth Huntington, *The Human Habitat*, D Van Nostrand Company, Inc (New York), 1927, p 15.

7. The Danish researcher Ole Fanger developed indices to quantify thermal comfort, beginning in the 1960s, of which the Predicted Mean Vote (PMV) is the most well known. Taking into account variables such as clothing, metabolic activity, air velocity and air temperature, the PMV is intended to predict whether a statistically large group of people will feel warm or cool under given environmental conditions. See P Ole Fanger, *Thermal Comfort – Analysis and Applications in Environmental Engineering*, Danish Technical Press (Copenhagen), 1970.

8. The CAV (Constant Air Volume) system was the standard until the 1970s. In this system, the air handler operates under steady-state conditions, and indiviudal room requirements are met by the use of secondary components such as reheat coils. In the VAV (Variable Air Volume) system, individual room requirements drive the air handler operation so that airflow rates can be significantly different throughout the building.

9. The 'Build Tight, Ventilate Right' phrase is a slogan of the Department of Energy's Energy Star programme. The premise is that building envelopes should be so tightly sealed that no outside air can penetrate. All the fresh air requirements are then met through the use of mechanical ventilation.

10. Reyner Banham, *The Architecture of the Well-Tempered Environment*, University of Chicago Press (Chicago, IL), 1984, p 19.

99.7 Per Cent Pure

The HEPA air filter is only capable
of processing 99.7 per cent of
airborne particles, leaving 0.3 per
cent unaccounted for. **Mason White**
describes the work of Canadian
installation artist An Te Liu who
made air-filtration appliances his
main subject.

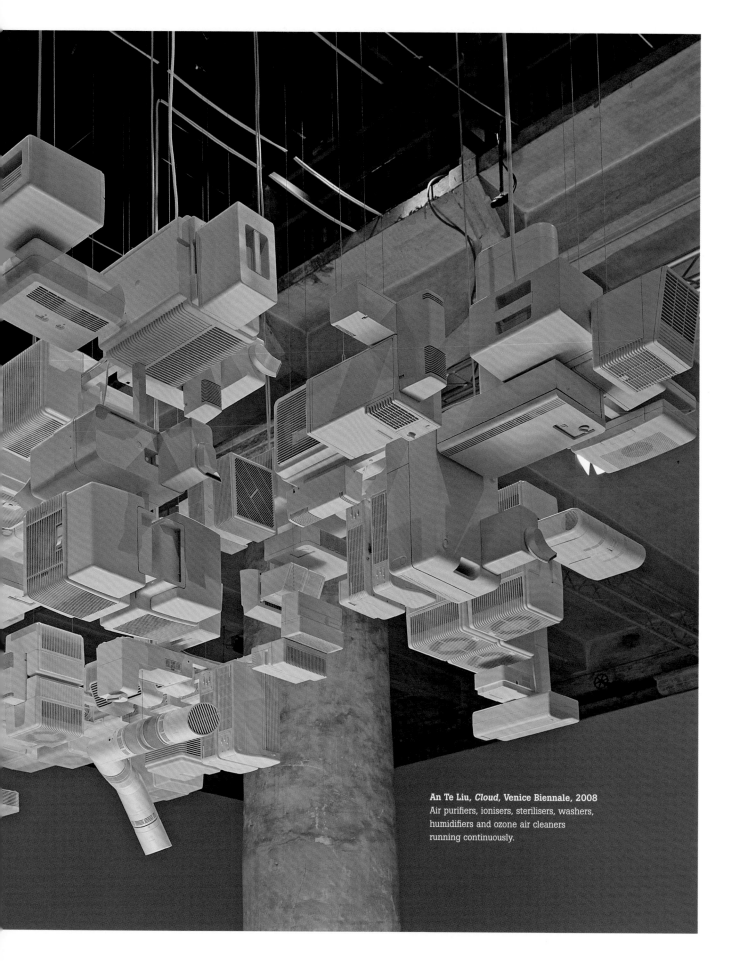

An Te Liu, *Cloud,* **Venice Biennale, 2008**
Air purifiers, ionisers, sterilisers, washers,
humidifiers and ozone air cleaners
running continuously.

Taiwanese-Canadian artist An Te Liu's recent work operates within the complex airspace of classification, hygiene and weightlessness. Charged with conflicting and multiple readings of scales and eras, Liu employs modified devices and materials in swarms and assemblies with a tenacious attention to sequencing. Since 2000, he has used a broad range of continuously running air-filtration appliances – from HEPA (high efficiency particulate air) filters to ozone air cleaners – in his work. The intention of this series of installations, which began with *Airborne*, is to stimulate our awareness of and increasing reliance on (or the promise of) filtered and purified air. Of course, like any quest for technological perfection, the devices reach a Zeno's-paradox-like impossibility. The HEPA filter, the most effective common domestic filtration product on the market, for example, is only capable of processing 99.7 per cent of airborne particulates, leaving a lingering concern surrounding the unaccounted for 0.3 per cent matter. Liu's filtration appliance series capitalises on this problem and its urban and architectural ramifications.

Innovations in air filtration originated from a desire for increased respiratory safety for fire fighters (in the 1820s), coal miners (in the 1850s) and, later, for underwater divers (1910s). Augustus Siebe's patented diving helmet used tubes and filters to pump fresh air in and bad air out. Siebe adapted this same system into the gas mask during the First World War. The HEPA filter was a wartime innovation in the 1940s, which effectively processed the air of US government scientists working in radioactive conditions. What began as a classified item later became a well-marketed and domesticated product. Over time, filtration technology continued to extend into the workplace and public institutions, offering some level of perceived atmospheric purity. And in recent decades, air modification has extended beyond the elimination of foul odours, toxicity and noxious gases to the removal of odourless and invisible elements such as viruses and bacteria.

Air-purification systems also developed in response to the increasing toxicity of building materials, cleaning products and bio-aerosols containing pathogens, formaldehyde, VOCs (volatile organic compounds), asbestos and lead. In the 1960s, Klaus and Manfred Hammes introduced the first residential air purifier in Germany, increasing awareness of the effects of these domestic substances. The 1970s energy crisis created catalytic conditions for the success of

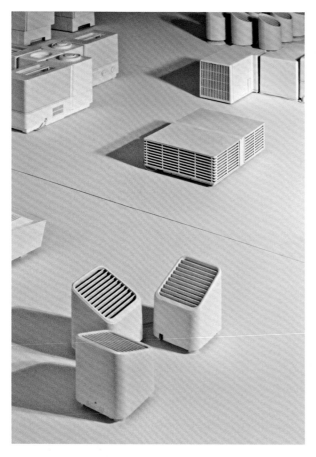

An Te Liu, *Airborne*, 2000
Air ionisers, purifiers, ecologisers, humidifiers;
64 units running continuously. Installation
view, Contemporary Art Gallery, Vancouver.

indoor air-filtration machinery, which sought to quarantine indoor from outdoor air. In 1984 the World Health Organization reported on a series of symptoms occurring at increasing frequencies in buildings with indoor climate issues. These symptoms, including irritation of the eyes, nose and throat, respiratory infections, dizziness and nausea later became known as Sick Building Syndrome (SBS). In Liu's air-filtration series, especially in *Airborne* (2000), *Exchange* (2001) and *Cloud* (2008), there is a seeming sickness in the excessive use of these appliances which are perpetually operational in such great numbers. Are the very machines designed to mitigate illness now in fact operating as facilitators of it? Air so pure, it hurts.

Inevitably wrapped up within their cultural status, Liu's appliance works also confront the complex evolution and development of their role within architecture and interiors. Early Modernism's faith in the technological agency in architecture predicted the significance to which it would influence building enterprises. Walter Gropius' 1956 *Scope of Total Architecture* posits a complete transformation of life 'brought about by technological

advancements' and, along with these changes, architecture that embodies a 'living urban organism' that he termed 'total architecture'.[1] In *Megastructures*, Reyner Banham offers the megastructure as a critique of Gropius' total architecture as being too homogeneous, culturally thin, and as dead 'as any other perfect machine'.[2] An Te Liu's work extends this critique from total architecture to megastructure. *Cloud* best exhibits this transition as it hovers effortlessly, teasing our airspace with its purity, a megastructure melding flocks of humming ionisers, purifiers and sterilisers, assembled in squadron formation, which aggregate into self-replicating and expanding clusters.

Liu's use of the appliance has shifted from the readymade to a modified unitised material. In *Cloud*, the appliances are merged, creating mutant assemblies and further confusing the scale at which the work is to be read. It is configurable, expandable and networked, and as a one-to-one reading it is intrusive – even excessive – highlighting the fear of unmediated interior environments. At an intermediate scale, the work is less Modernist urbanism than Futurist space-junk, since most of the material is intercepted by Liu, no doubt through online bartering portals, en route to dumps as the global e-waste burden grows. At its largest scale, *Cloud* is read as a machined

An Te Liu, *Exchange,* **2001**
above: HEPA air purifiers and cords; 56 units running continuously.
Installation view, Henry Urbach Gallery, New York.

An Te Liu, *Untitled* **(Complex IV), 2007**
above: Carpeting, Corian, distilled water, male and female pheromones,
vibrators and air sterilisers running continuously.

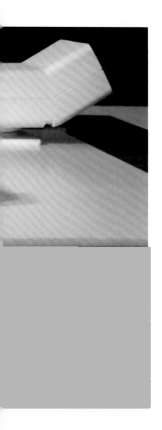

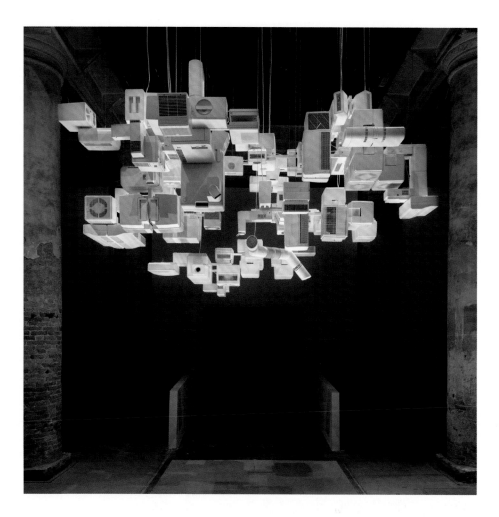

An Te Liu, *Cloud*, Venice Biennale, 2008
opposite bottom and right: Air purifiers, ionisers, sterilisers, washers, humidifiers and ozone air cleaners running continuously.

equivalent of an actual cloud abstracted into its components of moisture processing, air exchanges and atmospheric densities, and imagines the potential, as with snow-making machines, of generating entire weather conditions at will.

As with earlier works of the series, *Cloud* has had its overwhelming beige-ness traded for the cleanliness of white, and is fully operational. However, departing from static Brasilia-like assemblies, it hovers as if in mid-flight, embarking on a mission for space. Or perhaps it is a well-vented and exhaling space station – the ultimate megastructure. *Cloud* extends the ambition of levitation found in earlier works such as *Ether (or, Migratory Studies of the North American Chinatown)* (2004) in which rendered suburban fabric floats among cumulus-like cloud formations. In many ways its disposition is more akin to how we might conventionally think of mechanical systems: hung from the ceiling, tucked outside our more accessible visual field.

Installed at the 2008 Venice Biennale and acknowledging the inability to process or filter the entirety of the Arsenale, *Cloud* instead creates its own bubble of processed air dissipating into the larger space; an invisible zone of purity shape-shifting with the interior microclimates. Unlike earlier works with similar materials, *Cloud* is without orientation or reference. It has left the ground and thus left behind any reading of the Modernist city in favour of science fiction. Replacing the orderly plinth of *Airborne* and the columnar organisational logic of *Exchange*, its catenary-like suspension carries a new range of references grounded within 1960s architecture and 1970s film – perhaps Lando Calrissian's heady Cloud City from *The Empire Strikes Back*, or Yona Friedman's Ville Spatiale, a continuous space-frame with occupiable volumes. Either way, Liu's recent work seems to occupy the destabilising 0.3 per cent airspace where, given a tendency towards excess, there exists the slim margin that we are still not fully serviced by technological utopias. The processing and conversion of air into pure air, and its associated packaging, is caught between a Modernist ideal and a contemporary fear. ⏀

Notes
1. Walter Gropius, *Scope of Total Architecture*, Collier Books (New York), 1962.
2. Nigel Whiteley, *Reyner Banham: History of the Immediate Future*, MIT Press (Cambridge, MA), 2002, p 287.

'Never Mind All That **Environmental Rubbish,** Get On With Your Architecture'

Could the primacy of green architecture in recent years be eroding the discipline? Is it reducing architecture to a mere 'environmental techno-science'? **Penelope Dean** argues for a revised environmental agenda that is driven by ideas and concepts rather than subservient technologies.

Much of the ecologically motivated work today, acclaimed as green or contextual, is nothing more than a catalogue of environmental technology and land conservation systems tacked onto otherwise conventional buildings and landscapes.
– James Wines,[1] *l'ARCA*, September 1995, p 531

As architecture continues to be a target of environmental reform, the ambitions of the discipline have shifted from a Modernist notion of being able to design the environment to a subservient role as part of an environment by design. In this realignment, architecture's relationship to the environment has predominantly advanced through a combination of building and applied technology from the 1980s onwards, leading to a subcategory of architecture devolving into a kind of techno-science more commonly known as 'green architecture', or perhaps more accurately described as 'green building'. In this devolution the de-disciplining of architecture from a sociocultural project into a technological specialisation – the sustainable subculture where technology can apparently solve all problems – has taken place; in other words, a de-disciplining by shrinkage.

The premise of architecture's enviro-technological trajectory, a path indebted to the natural sciences and to a deeper disciplinary history dating from the late 1960s and early 1970s is that technological applications – for example, solar panels, photovoltaic cells, rainwater tanks – can address environmental concerns through a building's performance.[2] Driven by the notion that architecture should now do its ameliorative bit for the environment, 'sustainable design' or 'green architecture' – the latter referring specifically to 'the physical manifestation of environmental aspects in architecture'[3] – have become movements that, as Australian design theorist Tony Fry argued of the sustainability movement in general, are typically 'constituted as a discourse within the realm of technology', a discourse first deemed as the outcome of 'application technologies' and second 'as a metaphysic that installs a techno-functionalist way of

viewing the world'.[4] In this way, a dimension of architecture had been transformed into an environmental techno-science.

Of course no mention of technology in relation to the environment can begin without reference to the disciplinary contributions of R Buckminster Fuller and Reyner Banham during the late 1960s and early 1970s. One set of beginnings can be seen in the comprehensive design thinking of Fuller in his *Operating Manual for Spaceship Earth* of 1969. In this small book, Fuller gives a top-down, comprehensive diagnosis of the planet, one that he would parenthetically rename as 'Poluto', and one that he understands as a complete environment system.[5] In an extension of Modernist thinking and top-down planning, Fuller replaces the city with the world, where design – understood to include everything as a mission indebted to technology – should assume the task of generating advantage over adversity via 'accelerated scientific development' and systematic use of the computer.[6] Fuller called this 'design-science'.

A second underpinning, and one more directly related to architecture, appears in Reyner Banham's *The Architecture of the Well-Tempered Environment*, also of 1969, a book about the then underrated history of mechanical and lighting services. According to Banham, the 'Never mind all that environmental rubbish, get on with your architecture'[7] directive issued by those teaching architecture in British schools during the late 1960s was cause for concern. Grumbling about the failure of the architectural profession to assume adequate responsibility for environmental design in the book's introductory 'Unwarranted Apology', Banham argued that such neglect had led to 'another culture' consisting of plumbers and engineers appropriating the enviro-design field. In answer to what he saw as a problematic separation between architecture and technology vis-à-vis a building's performance,[8] he thus sought to reposition the importance of mechanical services and other environmental technologies to the centre of the discipline. Yet what Banham then diagnosed as an underrated disciplinary problem for architecture has since become an overzealous building-science problem, one often devoid of disciplinary concern, and one that has begun to subsume architecture.

Two of the clearest and most consistent articulations of the relationship between technology, architecture and the environment in the wake of Banham and Fuller come from Malaysian architect Ken Yeang's research into bioclimatic skyscrapers in Southeast Asia from 1981 onwards and, in the US, from architect William McDonough's

SITE Inc, Hialeah Showroom, Miami, Florida, 1979
In an extension of the surrounding landscape, a nature sample was grafted into an enclosed facade at the front of this BEST store. In 2005 James Wines of SITE retroactively noted that the Hialeah showroom represented not only their 'early use of vegetation and water as cooling elements in architecture', but also a 'commitment to green design'.

SITE Inc, Forest Building, Richmond, Virginia, 1980
In this BEST store, SITE conceived of nature as something to
be preserved, hyperbolised even, to give the appearance of
architecture being 'invaded and consumed by nature'.

use of sustainable materials and systems in buildings and
roofs dating from 1984 onwards. Yeang's theoretical
position resonates with Banham's enviro-science
ambitions: 'the design of energy-efficient enclosures has
the potential to transform architectural design from being
an uncertain, seemingly whimsical craft, into a confident
science,'[9] and Fuller's comprehensive design thinking:
'this energy equation in design is only part of a greater
gestalt in environmental design.'[10] From his Plaza Atrium
in Kuala Lumpur (1981–6), to Menara Mesiniaga in
Selangor (1989–92), Yeang's tall buildings have
responded to tropical climate conditions through a
combination of integrated vegetation in buildings, deep
air zones and wind-leeward facades. Closing what was for
Banham a problematic separation between architects and
'another culture', Yeang offers an inbred version that
closes the architecture-technology gap: environmental
design as the core of architecture.

Laying out what he calls 'Design Principles' in a series
of cartoon-like diagrams in his book *Bioclimatic
Skyscrapers* of 1994, Yeang provides an outline of the
role technology can play vis-à-vis architecture and the
environment. Beginning with a number of drawings
explicating the performance of external walls –
environmentally interactive walls, the attachment of
shading devices, balconies, terraces and vertical
landscaping to walls, insulative walls, solar-collector walls
and water-spray walls – Yeang's principles translate into
building facades as either 'clad in a ventilated rain-check
aluminium skin which traps heat and dissipates it'[11]
(Menara Boustead, 1986) or window areas whose 'faces
have external aluminium fins and louvers to provide sun
shading' or 'glazing details [that] allow the light-green
glass to act as a ventilation filter'[12] (Menara Mesiniaga).
Motivated by the natural sciences, Yeang's design

principles expose technology reduced to a wall application, and
architecture as a specialisation indebted to climatology.

In a slightly different approach, William McDonough, the
sustainability poster-child who brought ecologically intelligent design
to the mainstream through co-authored books such as *Cradle to Cradle*
(co-written with chemist Michael Braungart in 2002), has continued a
design-science agenda through explicit attention to the micro-technical
properties of building materials. In his earliest project, the executive
headquarters for the Environmental Defense Fund in New York
(1984–5), a project that McDonough himself described as 'the first of
the so-called green offices',[13] his internal environments reveal
architecture and technology to be an extension of materials science.
For example, when selecting interior finishings for the building he
writes: 'Of particular concern to us were volatile organic compounds,
carcinogenic materials, and anything else in the paints, wall coverings,
carpetings, floorings, and fixtures that might cause indoor air quality
problems or multiple chemical sensitivity.'[14] Designing interior
environments via the curation of materials, McDonough collapses
architecture and technology into a veneer – a normative surface
strategy (as opposed to Yeang's wall strategy) of techno-appliqué –
where selected materials are applied to planes in accordance with their
enviro-performance ratings.

McDonough's investment in surface and performance was later
exacerbated in a pallet of roofing materials and vegetation for his
retrofit (in collaboration with William Worn Architects) for a green roof
for Chicago's City Hall in 2001. Of green roofing in general he writes:
'It maintains the roof at a stable temperature, providing free
evaporative cooling in hot weather and insulation in cold weather, and
shields it from the sun's destructive rays, making it last longer. In
addition it makes oxygen, sequesters carbon, captures particulates like
soot, and absorbs storm water. ... In appropriate locales, it can even be
engineered to produce solar-generated electricity.'[15] Here, instead of
perceiving vegetation as a medium of landscape, McDonough conceives
it as just another technological surface, an applied infrastructure, now
curiously capable of generating solar electricity. In this context, the role

of architecture is marginalised as technological surfaces and performance criteria no longer serve the discipline per se, but rather the über-category of 'environment'.

The problem engendered by the techno-science trajectory to date – whether it be latent in the wall strategies of Yeang or manifested in the surface strategies of McDonough – is one that has seen a dimension of architecture privileging applied scientific solution over sociocultural projection or formal innovation. Despite numerous architectural publications continuing to promote techno-appliqué as the promising direction for green architecture,[16] it is also no surprise that such investments in architecture have seen their share of critique emerge from within the design fields, leaving many wondering if perhaps Banham's professors were right after all when they instructed: 'Never mind all that environmental rubbish, get on with your architecture.' Arguably one of the earliest critiques came from Italian engineer and design theorist Ezio Manzini in 1992 who stated that the role of design culture should not be a technological pursuit, but one that should rather 'advance a plurality of possibilities'.[17] Manzini writes:

> If science and technology march under the banner 'everything is possible', design culture must … point out a path for these potential possibilities, a path that can be completely opposed to that which technological-scientific development has followed up to now, a path whose scenarios prefigure results.[18]

Manzini's call for design culture to privilege a speculative agenda over a technological one was recently echoed inside architecture circles by founding SITE Inc member James Wines who, in his introduction to *Green Architecture* (2000), argued that the use of advanced technology in architecture for environmental solutions had tended to isolate the 'means from the mission'.[19] By 'mission', Wines referred to the 'conceptual, philosophical and artistic' ambitions of the discipline which he claimed were being lost in the wake of technological 'means' – his book was a subsequent attempt to reframe sustainable architecture through conceptual aspects.[20] If architecture's role used to lie in producing ideas and possible worlds for the environment during Modernism (that is, a prognostic role), the assessments of Manzini and Wines suggest that architecture has since been subsumed by a larger design world that aims to solve environmental problems (a reactive role). In this scenario, architecture is apparently able to do everything in direct proportion to its inability to think anything, the conflation of architecture and technology giving way to internal specialisation, paradoxically a focus to which Fuller (perhaps the most significant techno-enviro promoter) was always adamantly opposed. Significantly, this convergence has eroded architecture's capability to produce sociocultural design possibilities and alternatives.

What is at stake, therefore, is how the discipline might redirect and prioritise its ambitions in the context of an environment by design. Such a shift would not necessarily dismiss or eliminate the importance of environmental issues, but involve a change in mindset: a reorientation of architectural ambitions back towards the ends of a larger disciplinary agenda where the production of ideas and concepts would be reasserted, once again, as one of the central tasks of architecture. This agenda would require architecture to be understood

Emilio Ambasz, Prefectural International Hall, Fukuoka, Japan, 1992
Ambasz deploys landscape as a design medium through which to reinvent both nature and artifice. In 2004 he claimed to be the forerunner 'of current architectural production concerned with environmental problems'.

first and foremost as an intellectual discipline – a sociocultural practice – as opposed to an applied science, and would value technological advances as subordinate to the ends of an overarching disciplinary project. Rather than asking 'What can architecture do for green?', a reorientation of architecture's disciplinary concerns would seek to ask the politically incorrect question 'What can green do for architecture?'[21]

A starting point for a revised environmental agenda driven by ideas and concepts – and therefore a swerve away from the techno-science trajectory – might begin by recalling potential disciplinary points of departure from within architecture's history: for example, SITE's 'environmental sponge' ideas from the 1970s along with the conflation of landscape and architecture in their Hialeah, Terranium or Forest BEST showrooms (1978–80) might offer a way to rethink environmental walls; Emilio Ambasz's recasting of the 'soft over the hard' (vegetation over buildings) in his Green Town proposal for Japan (1992) suggests a way to rethink environmental surfaces; Clino Castelli and Andrea Branzi's late 1970s and early 1980s New Design experiments that sought to expand the limits of design through colour, decoration and materials propose a way to rethink environmental qualities independent of structural form; Le Corbusier's La ville verte (the green city) of 1929–30 with its encircling parks and rooftop cultures offers an early example of environmental urbanism; and finally, even the insights in Banham's chapter (entitled 'Concealed Power') on suspended ceilings in *The Architecture of the Well-Tempered Environment* could be appropriated for the formal interrogation of environmental sections. A re-examination of some of these propositions – if only as starting points – might just provide the necessary impetus to jump-start architecture with a more ambitious project, one capable of advancing a plurality of ideas and possible new worlds in an age of environmental concern. Δ

Notes
1. James Wines, 'Passages – A Changing Dialogue', in *I'ARCA*, No 96, September 1995, p 53.
2. Within the architecture discipline, RE Somol was one of the first to identify an alliance between a 'technological' architectural trajectory and sustainability. In 1993 he wrote that 'the discourses of technology and commodity' had promoted themselves 'as the movement for sustainability and community … Despite its claim to formal neutrality or disinterest, this renewed if self-serving alliance of the building and behavioral sciences (now expanding technology into the landscape and the examination of users beyond the given program) has nonetheless enforced a consistent (and constrained) form and vision.' See RE Somol, 'The Camp of the New', *ANY* 9, May/June 1993, p 55.
3. Wendy Meguro gave this definition in an interview with Jordan Kauffman in 'To LEED or Not to Lead', *Log* 8, Summer 2006, p 13.
4. Tony Fry, 'The Sustainment and its Dialectic', in *Design Philosophy Papers*, Team D/E/S Publications (Ravensbourne, Australia), 2004), p 33. For these reasons, sustainability, as Fry argues, was reduced to

Le Corbusier, Radiant City, 1929–30
opposite: Coincidently titled La ville verte (the green city), Le Corbusier's proposal for a city surrounded by parks with a rooftop culture consisting of 'sand beaches, clumps of shrubbery, and flowerbeds [...s]ur les toits de Paris' prefigures North American green city and green roof strategies.

Clino Trini Castelli, Gretl's Soft Diagram, 1977
below: Castelli's analysis of the Palais Stonborough's drawing room designed by Ludwig Wittgenstein in 1926. The diagram depicts hidden aspects of environmental organisations such as heating, sound, lighting and colour. Andrea Branzi included it as an example of Design 'Primario': a pursuit proposing the recovery and control of physical parameters in the design of interior environments.

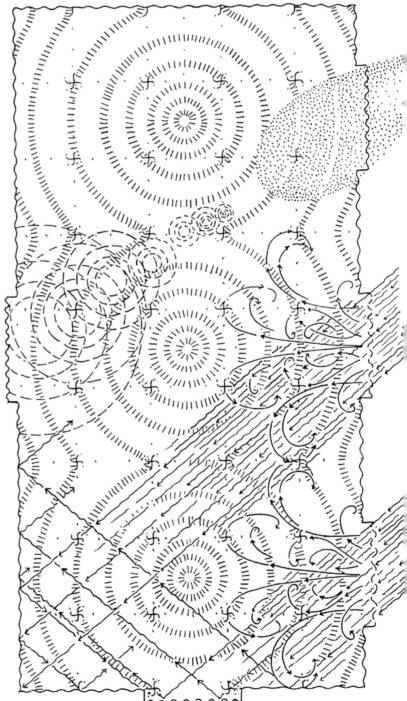

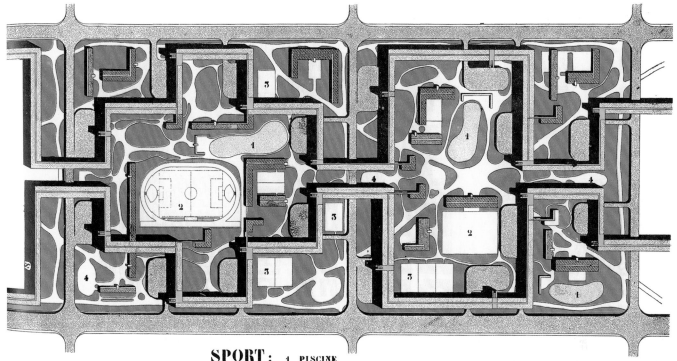

SPORT:
1 PISCINE
2 FOOTBALL, SAUT, ETC
3 TENNIS
4 JEUX

0   100   200

'instrumental action', giving rise to categories such as sustainable architecture, engineering and agriculture.

5. R Buckminster Fuller, *Operating Manual for Spaceship Earth*, Pocket Book edition (New York), 1970, p 70. First published by Southern Illinois Press in 1969.

6. See Chapter 8, 'The Regenerative Landscape', in ibid, pp 104–20.

7. Reyner Banham, *The Architecture of the Well-Tempered Environment*, The Architectural Press (London), 1984, 1st edn 1969, p 11. This sentence reappears in a slightly different version almost 20 years later as: 'Don't bother with all that environmental stuff, just get on with the architecture!' Quoted in Reyner Banham, 'A Black Box, the secret profession of Architecture', *A Critic Writes, Essays by Reyner Banham*, University of California Press (Berkeley and Los Angeles), 1996, p 295. This essay was first published in *The New Statesman in Society*, 12 October 1990.

8. Banham complained that the book was filed under 'technology' rather than 'architecture' in the school libraries, writing: 'The idea that architecture belongs in one place and technology in another is comparatively new in history, and its effect on architecture, which should be the most complete of the arts of mankind, has been crippling.' Banham, *The Architecture of the Well-Tempered Environment*, p 9.

9. Ken Yeang, *Bioclimatic Skyscrapers*, Artemis (London), 1994, p 17.

10. Ibid.

11. Ibid, p 43.

12. Ibid, p 59.

13. William McDonough and Michael Braungart, *Cradle to Cradle*, North Point Press (New York), 2002, p 8.

14. Ibid, pp 8–9.

15. Ibid, p 83.

16. For a compilation of recently realised projects following the technology trajectory, see Peter Buchanan's *Ten Shades of Green: Architecture and the Natural World*, The Architectural League of New York (New York), 2005. See also his 'Select Bibliography' at the back of this book.

17. Ezio Manzini, 'Prometheus of the Everyday: The Ecology of the Artificial and the Designer's Responsibility', in Richard Buchanan and Victor Margolin, *Discovering Design*, The University of Chicago Press (Chicago, IL), 1995, p 239. This paper first appeared in *Design Issues* 9, No 1, Fall 1992, pp 5–20.

18. Ibid, p 237.

19. James Wines, *Green Architecture*, Taschen (Milan), 2000, p 11. Wines went as far as to say in the book's concluding chapter that 'environmental architecture has become a camouflage to justify the work of some vociferously righteous, but very bad designers' (p 227).

20. As Wines writes in the book's introduction: 'While there are many publications today that cover the scientific and technological side of the eco-design revolution, this book approaches the subject from a conceptual, philosophical, and artistic perspective' (p 9). The book conversely received critiques for being insufficiently technical; see, for example, the annotated bibliography to Buchanan's *Ten Shades of Green* (2005). Additional criticisms of the technological trajectory can be found in Rosalie Genevro's preface to *Ten Shades of Green* (pp 4–5), and Michel Shellenberger's and Ted Nordhaus' essay 'The Death of Environmentalism: Global Warming Politics in a Post-Environmental World' of 2004 (www.thebreakthrough.org; accessed 31 March 2008). In this essay the authors argue that mainstream environmentalists have become too narrowly technical, having forsaken the task of imagining a better world. Another critique can be found in Mark Jarzombek's 'Sustainability: Fuzzy Systems and Wicked Problems' and Jordan Kauffman's 'To LEED or Not to Lead', *Log* 8, Summer 2006.

21. This is the subject of my essay 'Under the Cover of Green', in Dana Cuff and Roger Sherman (eds), *Fast Forward Urbanism: Designing Metrourban America*, Princeton Architectural Press (New York), forthcoming 2009.

This article is an edited excerpt from Chapter 8, 'Environment', of Penelope Dean's PhD dissertation entitled 'Delivery Without Discipline' (2008).

Meteorological

Philippe Rahm hails the emergence of a new meteorological architecture, in which the invisible takes precedence over the visible, and the atmospheric, conduction of heat, perspiration and shifting weather and climate conditions are foregrounded.

architecture

Philippe Rahm architectes,
Interior Gulf Stream, Research
House for Dominique Gonzalez-
Foerster, Paris, France, 2008

After decades devoted to the visible, in which a subjective approach and 'storytelling' shamelessly replaced the progressive and moral programmes of Modernity, we are now in a new and extremely interesting period. A slippage of the real from the visible towards the invisible is taking place, a shift of architecture towards the microscopic and the atmospheric, the biological and the meteorological. The considerable progress in life sciences resonates now with today's study of the climate and concerns of planetary warming. The field of the visible, until now saturated with symbols, morals, stories and individual

The tools of architecture must become invisible and light, producing places like free, open landscapes, a new geography, different kinds of meteorology; renewing the idea of form and use between sensation and phenomenon, between the neurological and the meteorological, between the physiological and the atmospheric.

interests, is in the process of deflating, deforming and de-programming. Unfurled from the dichotomies of the physiological and the climatic, between determinism and freedom, fluctuating and undetermined, this open field has become the space for a new humanist landscape.

As architects of these spaces, Philippe Rahm architectes aims to re-establish the language of architecture with the knowledge of this shift towards the invisible and to stretch architecture between the infinitely small and the infinitely large, between the physiological and the meteorological. The intention is to reposition the essence of the elements of architecture subsequent to this disintegration of the visible. The tools of architecture must become invisible and light, producing places like free, open landscapes, a new geography, different kinds of meteorology; renewing the idea of form and use between sensation and phenomenon, between the neurological and the meteorological, between the physiological and the atmospheric. These become spaces with no meaning, no narrative; interpretable spaces in which margins disappear, structures dissolve and limits vanish.

It is no longer a case of building images and functions, but of opening climates and interpretations; working on space, on the air and its movements, on the phenomena of conduction, perspiration, convection as transitory, and fluctuating meteorological conditions that become the new paradigms of contemporary architecture. It is necessary to move from metric composition to thermal composition, from structural thinking to climatic thinking, from narrative thinking to meteorological thinking. Space becomes electromagnetic, chemical, sensorial and atmospheric with thermal, olfactory and coetaneous dimensions within which we are immersed. The very act of inhabiting these spaces with the breath, perspiration and thermal radiation of our bodies in turn combines with this materiality; the physical environments of our surroundings. Between the infinitely small of the biological and the infinitely large of the meteorological, architecture must build unlimited sensual exchanges between the body and space, the senses, the skin, breath, the climate, temperature, or variations in humidity and light.

Advancements in the fields of the life sciences, molecular and genetic biology on one side and the increased interest in atmospheric issues arising from global warming on the other, provide a shift or, more specifically, an expansion of the spectrum of what constitutes reality, which today is perceived as a shift from the visible towards the invisible. Until now, the gestation processes of the city and buildings have produced petrified narratives, frozen forms of social, political and moral conventions. They have created fixed cultural landscapes that once opposed the natural, irrational fluctuation of the countryside and climate. Now, overtaken by progress and recent defeats by biology and atmospheric pollution, this dichotomy no longer exists. We can therefore reappropriate the tools of the natural to generate cities and buildings drained of their narrative, functionalism and determinism: buildings and cities that are then displayed as pure presences – fluctuating atmospheres, open, objective, 'non-adjectival' landscapes

Digestible Gulf Stream

Venice Biennale, 2008

Architecture should no longer build spaces, but rather create temperatures and atmospheres. The Digestible Gulf Stream is the prototype for architecture that works between the neurologic and the atmospheric, developing like a landscape that is simultaneously gastronomic and thermal. Two horizontal metal planes are extended at different heights. The lower plane is heated to 28°C (82.4°F), the upper one is cooled to 12°C (53.6°F). Like a miniature Gulf Stream, their position creates a movement of air using the natural phenomenon of convection, in which rising hot air cools on contact with the upper cool sheet and, falling, is then reheated on contact with the hot sheet, thus creating a constant thermal flow akin to an invisible landscape.

The interest here is the creation not of homogeneous, established spaces, but of a plastic, climatically dynamic activation of forces and polarities that generate a landscape of heat. In this case the architecture is literally structured on a current of air, opening up a fluid, airy, atmospheric space. This architecture is based on the construction of meteorology. The

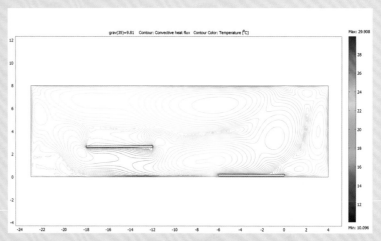

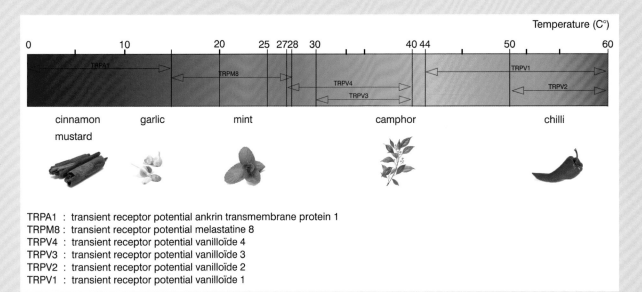

TRPA1 : transient receptor potential ankrin transmembrane protein 1
TRPM8 : transient receptor potential melastatine 8
TRPV4 : transient receptor potential vanilloïde 4
TRPV3 : transient receptor potential vanilloïde 3
TRPV2 : transient receptor potential vanilloïde 2
TRPV1 : transient receptor potential vanilloïde 1

inhabitant can move around in this invisible landscape at temperatures between 12°C and 28°C, the two extremities of the concept of comfort, and freely choose a climate according to his or her activity, clothing, dietary, sporting or social wishes. For example, when we feel too hot, we have five ways of cooling down, which act on different scales: 1) reducing the air temperature in the room, for example via air conditioning (atmospheric solution); 2) drinking (physiological solution); 3) taking off clothes (social solution); 4) resting (physical solution); 5) stimulating a sense of coolness with the mind (neurological solution). Each of these solutions is architecture. Architecture is a thermodynamic mediation between the macroscopic and the microscopic, between the body and space, between the visible and the invisible, between meteorological and physiological functions.

Adding two culinary/pharmaceutical preparations, which can be eaten or applied to the body, to the two planes directly stimulates the sensory receptors of hot and cold at the cerebral level. The first preparation, on the upper cold plane, contains mint, which has molecules of crystalline origin known as menthol that cause the same sensation in the brain as the coolness perceptible at a temperature of 15°C (59°F). The menthol activates the TRPM8 (transient receptor potential) molecular sensory receptors on the skin and in the mouth that stimulate the group of peripheral sensorial neurons known as cold-sensitive units. The second composition, on the lower hot plane, contains a mixture of chilli and camphor. In the chilli one of the molecules, capsaicin, activates the neuro-receptor TRPV1, which is sensitive to temperatures over 44°C (111.2°F). Mixed with camphor, it creates a sensation of 28°C (82.4°F) on the skin.

The traditional field of architecture thus expands, operating on both the atmospheric and gastronomic scales, breaking down the barriers between internal and external, body and space, neurology and physiology. The sensations of hot and cold may be perceived as much inside the body (diet) as outside (atmosphere). Architecture becomes a Gulf Stream that polarises the contrasts on different scales (hot/cold, low/high, clothed/unclothed, internal/external, rest/activity) to give rise to architecture as a convective movement of air, creating a place like geography, designing space like climate, atmosphere and gastronomy.

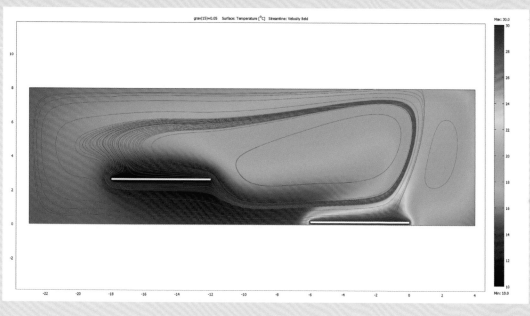

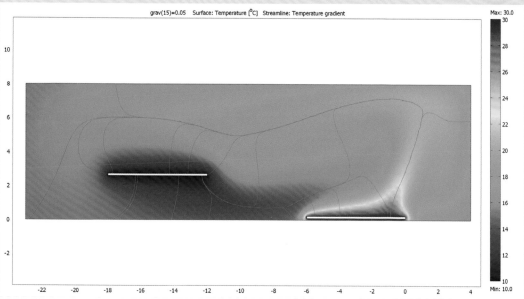

Mollier Houses

Vassivière en Limousin, France, 2005

The project for the Mollier holiday homes on Lake Vassivière reveals and characterises an invisible, yet essential, connection between interior space and humidity. It aims to transform a problem of building physics into an architectural question that informs the cause of its form, and introduces new sensual and physiological relations between the inhabitant, the space and the constraints of the technical equipment of the building. It engages closer ties with the lake landscape of Vassivière in Limousin, physical and chemical ties, as it is situated in the material character of the territory itself: humidity.

An occupant of an indoor space produces water vapour, not in a constant manner but according to the primary activity to which each room is dedicated. The presence of water vapour in the air originates naturally from respiration and hot water usage, leading to risks of condensation and damage to the construction. While today the only solution to excess interior water vapour is the common use of technical ventilation systems, the Mollier Houses project proposes shaping the space in relation to the water vapour in order to inaugurate a profound and complex relation between the inhabitants, their bodies, and the space according to its physical and chemical characteristics. Consequently, the architecture is designed, and the living spaces are given form, according to the variation of the relative humidity level, from the driest to the most humid, from 20 per cent to 100 per cent relative humidity. By means of the water vapour content, the quality of the architecture takes shape as the real and physical immersion of the inhabitants' bodies in the humid and variable body of the space.

Each house establishes a stratification of the levels of humidity within the space. A sleeping person emits around 40 grams (1.4 ounces) of water vapour per hour (bedroom) and produces up to 150 grams (5.3 ounces) per hour when active (living room). The use of a bathroom gives off up to 800 grams (28 ounces) in 20 minutes and the use of a kitchen, 1,500 grams (52.7 ounces) per hour. Like a set of Russian nesting dolls, the houses' living areas are designed according to the route of air renewal through the house, from the driest to the most humid, from the freshest to the stalest, from the bedroom to the bathroom. However, the project refuses to programme the space functionally according to specific activities, and instead creates spaces that are more or less dry, more or less humid, to be occupied freely, and to be appropriated according to the weather and the seasons.

The plan of the houses is a spatial representation of the Mollier diagram, creating new programmatic correspondences in which one space can receive several functions that are assumed to be separated. The driest room, between 0 per cent and 30 per cent relative humidity (RH) could be a drying room or a sauna. The next room, between 30 per cent and 60 per cent RH, could be a bedroom, an office or a living room. The third room, still more humid at between 60 per cent and 90 per cent RH, could be used as a bathroom, a living room or a kitchen. The last room, the most humid at between 90 per cent and 100 per cent RH, could be used as a living room or a pool. However, none of the rooms are specifically determined by a function. They remain freely appropriable according to the level of humidity sought.

The project also amplifies the hydrometric layering of the landscape, integrating both the physical presence of the lake water and the natural exterior humidity as if it were a room in the house with a humidity level of 100 per cent. The buildings are arranged linearly, positioned along a pre-existing incline of natural terrain, engulfed by the waters of the artificial lake.

ventilation system

relative humidity 100%   relative humidity 90%   relative humidity 70%   relative humidity 30%   relative humidity 10%

Interior Gulf Stream, Research House for Dominique Gonzalez-Foerster

Paris, France, 2008

The thermodynamic phenomenon of the Gulf Stream is one of the most fascinating models for thinking about architecture today in that it gives a route to escape from the normalisation and the homogenisation of the modern space. Modernity led to uniform, consistent spaces in which the temperature is regulated around 21°C (69.8°F). The aim of the Interior Gulf Stream project is to restore diversity to the relationship that the body maintains with space, with its temperature, to allow seasonal movement within the house, migrations from downstairs to upstairs, from cold to warm, winter and summer, dressed and undressed. For people to feel comfortable in a heated room there must be equilibrium in the exchange of heat occurring via convection between their bodies and the surrounding air. This equilibrium is of course relative to clothing, from nudity in the bathroom, to the thermal protection of blankets, to light clothing worn in the living room. Today, confronted with the need to preserve our energy resources, it is necessary to set each building, and even each room within building,s to a precisely calculated thermal capacity (based on the Swiss construction norm SIA 3842, which gives indicative values for ambient temperature) in order to expend only the energy that is strictly necessary: bathroom 22°C (71.6°F); living room 20°C (68°F); kitchen 18°C (64.4°F); bedrooms 16°C (60.80°F); hallways, toilet 15°C (59°F).

The project consists of an asymmetrical distribution of heat in the house, creating a convection movement in the entire space as two radiators are extended at different heights across the diagonal of the house. The lower radiator is heated to 28°C (82.4°F), and the upper one cooled to 12°C (53.6°F). The shape of the house is formed from the resultant thermal movement of the model. The inhabitants move around in this invisible landscape between the two temperatures, which are commonly accepted as the two ends of the spectrum of comfort, therefore freely choosing a climate to suit their different activities. The spaces within the house are plastic and climatically dynamic, generating a landscape for various uses that is structured by currents of air.

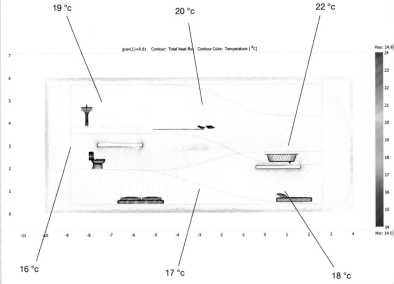

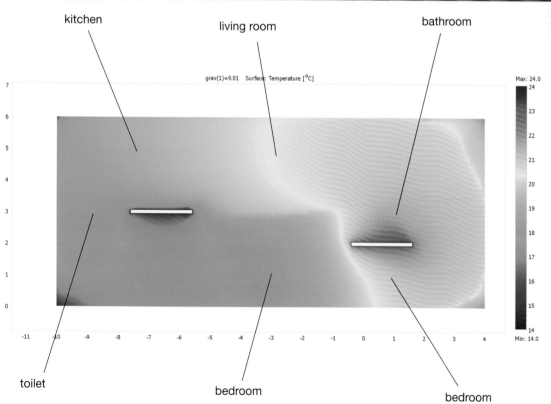

kitchen

living room

bathroom

grav(1)=9.81   Surface: Temperature [°C]

Max: 24.0

Min: 14.0

toilet

bedroom

bedroom

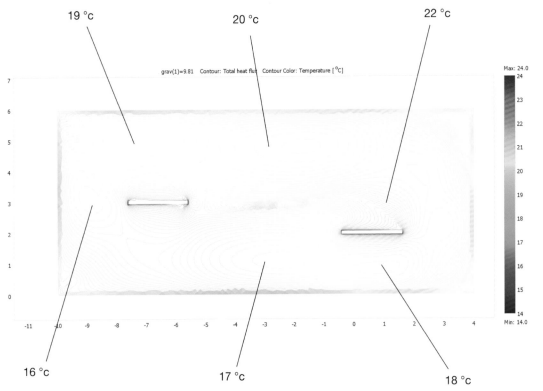

19 °c   20 °c   22 °c

grav(1)=9.81   Contour: Total heat flux   Contour Color: Temperature [°C]

Max: 24.0

16 °c   17 °c   18 °c

that we inhabit, thus interpreting them. Architecture becomes a new atmosphere and a second meteorology, no longer the 'subjective' closed place of social and political relationships, but instead an 'objective' open place where new social and political relationships can be invented.

In his letter to Pope Leo X at the beginning of the 16th century (1519), the painter Raphael explains the distinctive nature of the architect's representational techniques by comparing them to those of the painter, the plan being most important for the architect in the same way that perspective was the most essential mode of

Architecture is the creator of typologies and the creator of plans, including the materialities that make up the plan and activities that occur within it. Perhaps, then, perspective will follow. Rather than the 'architectural project', the preference is instead for the notion of the 'project of the architectural project' or the 'architecture of the project'.

representation for the painter: 'The drawn plan, belonging within the realm of the architect, is different from the painter's drawing.' Raphael essentially adopts the distinction between architecture and painting made by Leon Battista Alberti, which claimed for the architect the drawn plan and prohibited the use of the perspective drawing, which was to be used exclusively by the painter.

It seems vital that we return to this fundamental distinction, to the plan and its creation, as the essential starting point of our work, preceding all other types of representation: this is an exploration within the very matrix of architectural form and its spatial organisation, at the heart of its most fundamental tenets and terminology. The history of architecture is marked by this sort of foundational moment, which can be misunderstood as being merely a return to the plan as the basis for architectural representation. But it is instead how the plan allows for a fundamental re-evaluation of architectural language and principles, as well as providing a necessary platform from which to periodically rearticulate its implications. This renewed focus on the plan drawing and resulting reinvigoration of the discourse around architectural language appears to be a necessary process during periods when the rhetoric of the theoretical realm eclipses and clouds the more relevant issues of the moment. This academicism results in a certain stagnation, where its multitude of ideas and perspectives are in reality outcomes of a very singular type of plan; coming forth from the same mould, from the same specific frame of mind that we inevitably begin to take for granted.

The plan drawing is thus the original form of representation of the architect, and the development of a new sort of plan is required. The idea of the 'architectural project' can be a trap, as it fails to question the fundamental substance of the plan drawing and of architectural form itself; it leans too heavily on a predetermined language, all the while seducing us with a certain richness of expression and form, merely a consequence of contextual multiplicity. The methodology behind the architectural project is essentially one of a singular rhetoric applied in different contexts, which is what gives it a false impression of multiplicity and adaptability. Architecture is the creator of typologies and the creator of plans, including the materialities that make up the plan and activities that occur within it. Perhaps, then, perspective will follow. Rather than the 'architectural project', the preference is instead for the notion of the 'project of the architectural project' or the 'architecture of the project'.

The task of the work included here is to invent a new sort of plan, to formulate new sorts of typologies within the realms of meteorology and physics, articulating the movements of air, the transformation of water into vapour, the rates of renewal of a mass of air, sound pressures, temperature and respiration, perspiration and metabolism – creations stemming from the search for a new sort of plan as a literal, unexpected and jubilant result of the design process. ᐃ

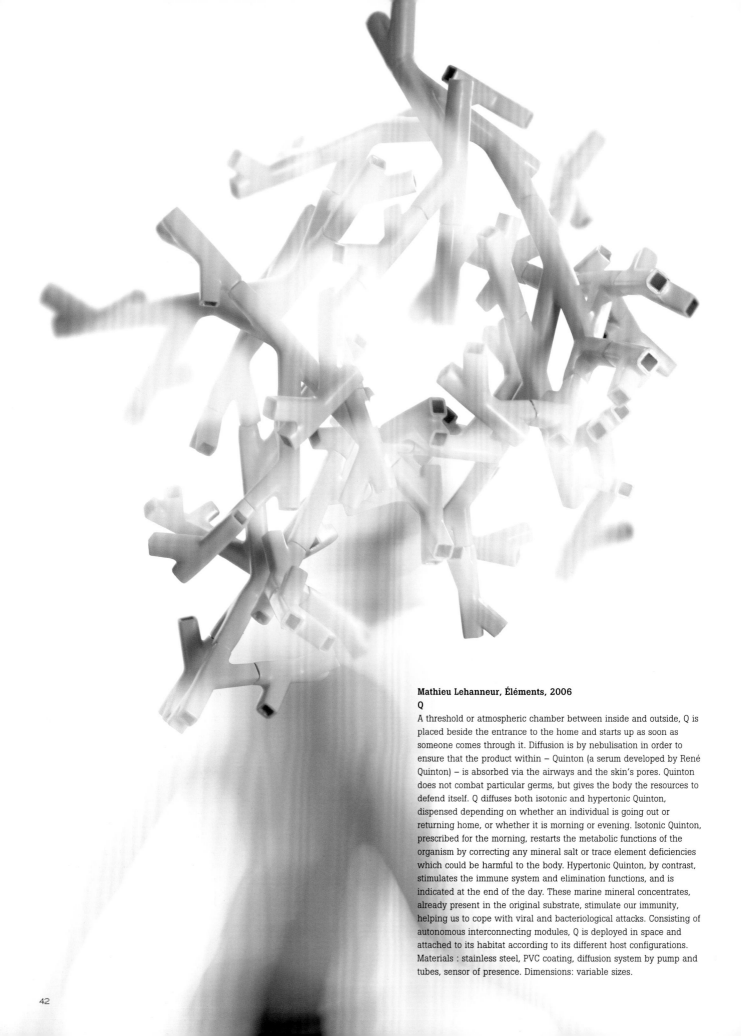

Mathieu Lehanneur, Éléments, 2006

Q

A threshold or atmospheric chamber between inside and outside, Q is placed beside the entrance to the home and starts up as soon as someone comes through it. Diffusion is by nebulisation in order to ensure that the product within – Quinton (a serum developed by René Quinton) – is absorbed via the airways and the skin's pores. Quinton does not combat particular germs, but gives the body the resources to defend itself. Q diffuses both isotonic and hypertonic Quinton, dispensed depending on whether an individual is going out or returning home, or whether it is morning or evening. Isotonic Quinton, prescribed for the morning, restarts the metabolic functions of the organism by correcting any mineral salt or trace element deficiencies which could be harmful to the body. Hypertonic Quinton, by contrast, stimulates the immune system and elimination functions, and is indicated at the end of the day. These marine mineral concentrates, already present in the original substrate, stimulate our immunity, helping us to cope with viral and bacteriological attacks. Consisting of autonomous interconnecting modules, Q is deployed in space and attached to its habitat according to its different host configurations. Materials : stainless steel, PVC coating, diffusion system by pump and tubes, sensor of presence. Dimensions: variable sizes.

Domestic Micro-Environments

In the following works, **Mathieu Lehanneur** readdresses our understanding of domestic spaces through the environmental systems that control and condition them. Such spaces are generally conditioned by centralised heating, cooling and ventilation systems that lump together many sensory qualities, including primary thermal controls as well as by-products of scent and sound, into a singular, mechanical system that fails to engage any of them fully. Lehanneur's projects look to separate these senses into systems distributed throughout the home, engaging each one specifically and locally, in an attempt to redefine the domestic spaces they are located within.

Mathieu Lehanneur, Éléments, 2006
dB
Very much like a household pet, dB moves around like a rolling ball. It constantly captures the sound level of its habitat, and as soon as it considers that the volume of noise is unacceptable it moves into a position as close as possible to the source of the noise, whether it is a crying child or a TV set. It can also position itself beside a window if it considers outside noise to be too loud. In all cases, it continuously emits the manufactured sound known as white noise, which is the sum of all frequencies that are audible to the human ear, brought to the same intensity. While noise is a cause of disruption, the advantage of white noise lies in the fact that it creates a band of sound whose lesser intensity enables the brain to adjust to it, and to no longer be disturbed by outside nuisance. It is no accident that some people claim to sleep very peacefully beside a waterfall, since the sound it creates is very similar to white noise. Materials: ABS, mini speakers, electric engine, charger. Dimensions: diameter 18 cm.

Mathieu Lehanneur

Éléments

2006

We do not live in sealed compartments. Our body and its immediate environment form a whole in which a multitude of exchanges take place: thermic, gaseous, sonorous. This state of immersion is responsible for both our subsistence and our equilibrium, but it also represents a danger. Our body is in a permanent state of adaptation: each change to any external parameter activates a function that enables it to adjust. We are continually in a state of hyper-reactivity. The pupil retracts in reaction to light, gooseflesh appears when we are cold – these are just two visible signs. But, in a more discreet way, some external input changes us deeply and can trigger fatigue and reduced vigilance and affect our health or even our strength.

Éléments intends to inverse this process. The elements no longer oblige the body to adapt but, on the contrary, generate domestic micro-environments dedicated to each inhabitant. They produce a kind of intangible food that is deployed using the principle of permanent capture of the parameters of the domestic environment of the inhabitants – light, air quality, background noise, body temperature, movements. This works as a series of discrete instances with a principle of instantaneous modification to existing parameters in order to adapt them as near as possible to our needs. Based on ancestral or contemporary research into the effects of various physical agents, the general intention of Éléments is to develop a home that is similar to the epidermis, reactive and capable of sensitivity to, and receptivity of, human states that is so acute that it can react precisely and quickly, and indeed faster than our own body. Posted in a constant state of alert, the Éléments work entirely autonomously, each establishing a map of its field of investigation and responding to it.

C°

Our body is not evenly maintained at 37°C (98.6°F), and for us to survive only our vital core – our heart and our brain – need to achieve this temperature constantly. Our extremities can easily fall to 25°C (77°F). The C° element acts like an intelligent camp fire at the heart of a room. It has the ability to perceive these temperature variations in bodies close to it, and emits a localised infrared heat towards these different zones, without knowing whether they are a part of one individual or parts of different bodies, such as two hands belonging to two different people beside one another. Like a permanent thermal radar, C° only emits heat towards one zone at a time. Thus, if it is surrounded by three people and someone else comes in from the cold, C° leaves them to concentrate exclusively on the new arrival, until his or her temperature reaches that of the others present.

Materials: elastomer, thermic camera, infrared heating, memory-shape alloy.

Dimensions: height 25 cm, diameter 66 cm.

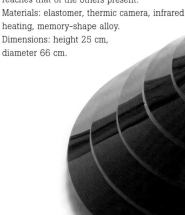

O

A veritable domestic breathing machine, O generates pure oxygen in the home. In big towns, oxygen levels are 90 per cent lower than those required by our bodies under optimal conditions. Using an oximeter sensor, O constantly monitors the oxygen level in the air, and when it detects that this level is insufficient it instantly activates the micro-organisms it contains – *Spirulina platensis*, a living organism with the highest yield in terms of oxygen production – and a light that favours spirulin photosynthesis. This emits native oxygen, which is diffused into its surroundings. As soon as the air oxygen level has returned to optimum, the light and agitation are interrupted and the spirulin falls back to the bottom of the container. NASA is currently carrying out very detailed studies of this subject in relation to long-term trips for its astronauts.
Materials: glass, aluminium, *Spirulina platensis,* magnetic stirrer, white LEDs, oxymetric probe.
Dimensions: height 47 cm, diameter 42 cm.

K

Our biorhythm, based on alternating day and night, is regulated by the pineal gland, located in the brain. It activates or stops the secretion of melatonin, our natural sleep-inducer, putting us into a state of vigilance or rest, which is a very simple way of explaining why we feel energetic during the day and why we want to sleep at night. If the light is insufficient in winter, for example, K, which is parameterised for activation according to the light received during the previous 24 hours by its capillary tubes, all of which are absorbable light sensors, determines our requirements in terms of reconstituted sunlight. It starts up only when one sits down in front of it, as one would in front of a crystal ball, and emits a very strong light – 10,000 lux in this case – for a period of a few seconds up to several minutes. Any light deficit has repercussions for humans, ranging from reduced energy or reduced libido, right through to states of depression.
Materials: aluminium, sheated optical fibres, photoelectric cells, high-luminosity white LEDs, sensor of presence. Dimensions: height 30 cm, length 28 cm. Scale: 1 : 28 cm.

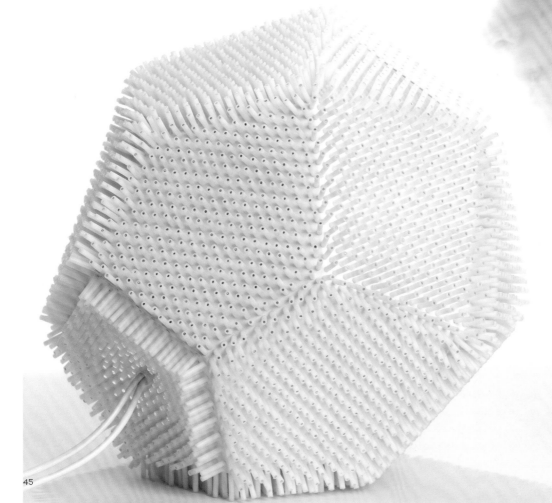

Mathieu Lehanneur with Anthony van den Bossche

Local River, Artists Space

New York, 2008

The term 'Locavore' was coined in the San Francisco Bay area in 2005 by a group who define themselves as 'culinary adventurers who eat foods produced within a radius of 100 miles [160 kilometres] around their city'. Their ultimate aim is to reduce the impact of the transportation of foods on the environment while ensuring their traceability.

Mathieu Lehanneur and Anthony van den Bossche's Local River project anticipates the growing influence of this group (the word 'locavore' made its first appearance in an American dictionary in 2007) by proposing a home storage unit for live freshwater fish combined with a mini vegetable patch. This DIY fish farm cum kitchen garden is based on the principle of aquaponics coupled with the exchange and interdependence of two living organisms – plants and fish. The plants extract nutrients from the nitrate-rich dejecta of the fish, and in so doing act as a natural filter that purifies the water and maintains a vital balance for the ecosystem within which the fish live. The same technique is used on large-scale pioneer aquaponics/fish farms that raise tilapia (a food fish from the Far East) and lettuce planted in trays floating on the surface of ponds.

Local River responds to everyday needs for fresh food that is 100 per cent traceable. It bets on a return to favour of farm-raised freshwater fish (trout, eel, perch, carp and so on) given the dwindling supplies of many saltwater species due to overfishing, and also demonstrates the capacity of fish farmers to deliver their stock live to a private consumer as a guarantee of optimum freshness – impossible in the case of saltwater fish that have been netted. The intention is to replace the decorative 'TV aquarium' with an equally decorative but also functional 'refrigerator aquarium'. In this scenario, fish and greens cohabit for a short time in a home storage unit before being consumed by their keepers, the end players, in an exchange cycle that takes place within a controlled ecosystem. ⌂

Local River creates a closed system of food production and waste between the vegetation and plants above and the fish living below before both are eventually consumed. Materials: blown and thermoformed glass, water pump, joints. Dimensions: large 163.7 x 76.7 x 101cm, small 76.7 x 46.2 x 92.4 cm.

Breeding the Future

For **Zbigniew Oksiuta** energy from the sun offers the greatest potential for architecture, as the essential life-giving force for all living things. Here he urges a future of architecture that is biological, as demonstrated by his own featured bioforms that investigate the cultivation of new types of organisms and living biological products outside the confines of natural evolution.

Zbigniew Oksiuta, Biological Habitat, Form 280807,
Prix Ars Electronica, Linz, Austria, 2007
Polymer wisps on the surface of the hollow sphere emerge
via self-made processes at the molecular level during the
drying process and constitute the 3-D construction web of
a naturally evolved filmy membrane.

**Zbigniew Oksiuta, Spatium Gelatum: Form
090704, Venice Biennale, 2004**
right and opposite top: Form 090704 after
several spatial invaginations and deformations.
Chaotic curves, deformations and invaginations
of the polymer sphere are the effect of precise
biological self-organisation processes combining
the physical and chemical principles of order
and beauty in the animated world.

From the dawn of mankind, humans have used biological
matter to separate and protect themselves from their
adverse environment. The construction of a spatial
boundary between surroundings and interior is the basic
task of architecture. Like the creation of cellular
membranes in biological systems, the making of clothes
or the construction of a roof over one's head are universal
and primeval activities, a condition of survival, for
existence and development. However, in order to build a
house, or make a pair of shoes, it is necessary to cut down
a tree, or to tear off the skin of an animal. Our modern
industry uses increasingly fewer materials of direct
biological origin. Unfortunately the costs of the new
technologies are incomparably higher, and a global mega-
organism – the biosphere – is the unfortunate victim.[1]

'Housing as shelter is an extension of our bodily heat-
control mechanisms – a collective skin or garment.'[2] It is
a natural, physiological assignment. Although in the
language of civilisation we continue to talk about 'growth'
and 'development', these terms 'have nothing to do with
the natural processes of development. Here nothing
grows, but rather materials are exploited and used to
produce, build and construct dead objects. Their common
feature is that they are not alive.'[3] In our minds, 'What is
living is too flawed to be used in structures, whereas what
is lifeless lives through the fact that it is permanent.'[4]

The transformation of man from when he was solely a
hunter and gatherer to the introduction of agriculture
10,000 years ago, was the beginning of biotechnology.
The decision to kill an animal for its meat for direct use,

or to keep it alive as a tool for breeding other animals or vegetation,
was a historical turning point. In modern biotechnology, plants and
animals are no longer viewed nostalgically as nature, or as a source of
biomass, but as extraordinary living 'tools' with the ability to breed
other organisms. However, the development of biological sciences,
especially genetics, will in future allow us to go a step further, to create
new tools outside natural evolution for the breeding of until now
unknown organisms and biological products. The cultivation of plants
and animal products for our consumption could then occur within
these new semibiological systems without victimising living organisms.

Though we continue to build tools, machines and houses that
remain as dead objects, for the last half a century we have begun to
better understand the biological processes of life: the flow of matter,
energy and information. This wisdom will one day allow us to create
objects, machines or architectural structures not only from dead
materials such as metal, concrete or plastic, but also through growing
them in biological ways. Soon we will be able to create a new
'replicator' that will open the way for a new evolution – a hybrid
between nature and culture occurring at speeds previously unheard of.

Using the creative potential of earthly matter, evolution has worked
out methods for survival and development that greatly exceed the brief
experience of mankind. These methods are based on smooth processes
and are the opposite of our 'permanent' constructions. Life is a
biochemical process occurring on a molecular scale. Biochemical
processes can only take place in unstable matter that enables free
movement and the exchange of molecules. Such matter is provided by
water and semiliquid, sticky protoplasm, and for these processes to be
at all possible it is necessary to separate protoplasm from its
environment. Over billions of years, evolution has developed a universal
biologic membrane, a fluid partition that effectively protects the

Zbigniew Oksiuta, Spatium Gelatum, Form 191202, International Furniture Fair, Cologne, Germany, 2003
Spatium Gelatum technology studies the rules for forming liquid and congealed 3-D membranes from biological polymers. PVC balloons rotate the liquid mass in flexible, sphere-shaped forms. As the object is rolled on the surface of the water, the liquid polymer inside it is mixed. As it cools, the mass is converted into a gel state, settling on the inner surface and forming a congealed membrane.

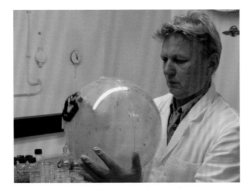

Zbigniew Oksiuta, Breeding Space, Botanical Institute of the University of Cologne, Germany, 2006
Forming an agar layer in the 3-D bioreactor and preparation of the sphere for growing organisms within. The transparent agar membrane contains all the substances necessary for a self-sustaining miniature world.

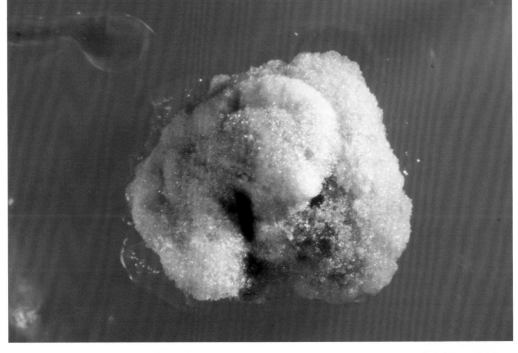

Zbigniew Oksiuta, Transgenic Habitat, Uncontrolled Biological Growth, Max Planck Institute for Plant Breeding Research, Cologne, Germany, 1990
A callus, a shapeless mass of non-differentiated and rapidly dividing cells. Recorded examples demonstrate natural genetic techniques used by microbes to disturb the natural rules of development and to cause morphological anomalies and deformations. The project studies the possibilities of using the DNA code for creating new plant objects.

Part of a sterile plant callus culture showing white embryogenic structures, pale leaves and transparent root tips. Providing uncontrolled processes with a spatial structure on the polymeric 3-D spheres and scaffolds, created using Spatium Gelatum technology, could enable the development of new plant spaces in architectural dimensions.

Zbigniew Oksiuta, The Cosmic Garden, Random Positioning Machine (in motion), Centre for Contemporary Art, Ujazdowski Castle, Warsaw, Poland, 2007
The Cosmic Garden project is a universal self-sustaining system in space, containing organisms in a transparent polymer sphere that interact and survive using solar energy. The Random Positioning Machine is a device for simulating microgravity and studying the sensitivity of organisms to the impact of gravity (geotropism). The rotating spherical bioreactor in the middle of the machine is a model of the Cosmic Garden in its weightless condition.

precious contents of every living cell so that these biochemical processes can take place.[5] Because they are unstable, such processes have enormous potential for development, thus their evolution can be based on coincidence, and physical and chemical instincts instead of conscious decisions. The instability of living systems makes for the stability of evolution.

The work featured here acts as a crossover between architecture, art, and biological and space sciences. The general aim of the research is to create the conditions for the development of a biological habitat, as a kind of 3-D bioreactor. The projects thus examine dynamic systems that transfer information and energy through liquid mediums, using biological polymers as building materials to develop liquid, jelly-like and rigid 3-D membranes at a human scale under different gravitational conditions: on earth, under water and in space. The membranes are used as a scaffolding for the growing of plant tissues and as biological fabricators for breeding plant objects to create conditions for plant biological systems that use the energy of the sun for the breeding of semiliving objects.

In the near future, the processes of creating will be decentralised, occurring biologically and on site without the need for the global transport of materials and tools. Only information will act globally, as 'matter' will transform locally. Energy from the sun will activate information embedded in the living matter in the bioreactors to start biological self-organisation processes, which will be controlled by global information – a new kind of 'biological Internet' that will encapsulate our

planet. This will have unforeseen consequences for our civilisation, as it has the potential to change our social and economic structures, including our systems of producing, distributing and using energy.

This vision has nothing to do with our familiar, romantic notion of nature. Each of us will be the owner of a personal biological fabricator connected to our body that will permit us to breed the things we need. As an incubator or artificial womb, this new extension of the body might have different dimensions – the size of a cell, a pill, a fruit, a house or even a biosphere – and, as the new cradle of life, allow us to cultivate food, tools and new shelters. 'The Future of life may exist only inside ecological enclosures, a kind of biological miniaturized world.'[6] Such personal biological 'replicators' could be miniature biospheres. They could even be sent into space, as universal sperm, to inseminate the cosmos with life. **⌀**

Notes
1. See Zbigniew Oksiuta, 'Forms, Processes, Consequences', Exhibitions catalogue, Arsenal Gallery, Bialystok, and Centre for Contemporary Art, Ujazdowski Castle, Warsaw, 2007.
2. Marshall McLuhan, *Understanding Media: The Extensions of Man*, Mentor Books (New York), 1964, p 117.
3. Herbert Gruhl, *Das irdische Gleichgewicht*, Deutscher Taschenbuch Verlag (Munich), 1985, p 22.
4. Ernst Bloch, *Das Prinzip Hoffnung*, Suhrkamp Verlag (Frankfurt), 1959, p 844. (The Principle of Hope, MIT Press 1995.)
5. Zbigniew Oksiuta, op cit.
6. Dorion Sagan, *Biospheres: Reproducing Planet Earth*, Bantam Books (New York), 1990, p 8.

When Cold Air Sleeps

Our cities today can be read off in binary contrast, as a 'figure- ground' of conditioned and unconditioned spaces. What, however, if we stopped regarding the outside as something to be tempered or mediated? Guest-editor **Sean Lally** of WEATHERS explains how for his practice climatic conditions open up new potential for organisational and spatial design.

WEATHERS in collaboration with Morris Architects, Estonian Academy of Arts, Tallinn, Estonia, 2008
Photo with the facade removed showing the Artificial Climatic Lungs positioned between the floor plates above and the public park below.

Giambattista Nolli's 1748 map of the city of Rome was of particular importance for the time in the way it represented the entire city as an architectural plan, delineating the semipublic spaces of churches, theatre interiors, courtyards and stairways in the same white notation as public streets, and thus demarcating a continuously accessible public space. It was this reading of the city, creating a map that reinforced a dichotomy through the black-and-white representation of public and private spaces, that was so unique. If we were to map our cities today, showing not the walls and envelopes, but rather the artificially conditioned, climate-controlled (primarily interior) spaces versus what we view as the intentionally unaltered (exterior) context, we would see as striking a dichotomy of figure-ground as we see in Nolli's 18th-century map. When the city is viewed not as public versus private space, but as conditioned versus unconditioned space, the surfaces and geometries of architecture are often coincident with, and responsible for fortifying, these boundaries.

Facilitating this binary contrast is not only our construction of the surfaces and walls that control this distinction and separation, but also our reluctance, as designers, to engage the climatic context that exists outside these surfaces as anything more than a condition to be tempered or mediated, a condition beyond the scope of design control. In contrast, the work by WEATHERS included here seeks an augmentation and redesign of 'nature' itself (which we all know to be anything but natural). It acknowledges an opportunity to operate upon the climate-conditioned and augmented materialities that make up our context, removing the coincidental relationship of a building's surfaces and walls from the artificial climates we compose within them.

The lines and surfaces architects create and rely on ensure that the potential spatial typologies and behaviours of these 'material energies' are never really given any responsibility other than predefined comfort control. Walls and surfaces essentially serve to cap their behaviours, preventing them from operating to their fullest potential or embracing their inherent proclivities as possible thresholds, circulation strategies or physical boundaries. All will inevitably influence social organisations and spatial typologies if given the chance. These gradient boundaries and strategies pertain not only at the local building scale, but also within the larger urban and regional constructions, influencing the organisational principles of our domestic, civil and commercial spaces.

The lines and surfaces of architecture must give way to gradients if we are to look to alternative design methods and strategies for articulating and operating upon this broader spectrum of materiality. Thresholds exist not only as lines and surfaces, but also as intensities, accumulations and gradients – the inherent properties of the spatial distribution of temperature, scent and light. Such thresholds engage a broader vocabulary within our sensory system, one beyond that of eyesight. By shifting our conceptualising of boundaries away from surfaces and lines, we see how such gradient boundaries newly inform and shape our spatial definition and organisation. Even with today's visualisation software capabilities, GIS and satellite mapping technologies that scan, simulate and quantify the multiple networks, infrastructure and layered communications that make up our cities and speckle the global landscapes, none alone can overcome the striking black-and-white dichotomy of the artificially conditioned spaces of our interiors versus the climatic conditions and underutilised materialities these interiors nest within. This is not an attempt to remap the city, but rather to instigate operations at the scale of local conditions in the knowledge that the implications will seep out and inform the larger world.

Too often associated with interiority, such materialities do in fact extend beyond the envelopes of domestic, commercial and institutional buildings. And when they do, their responsibilities must increase and adapt. Numerous examples illustrate this, most no more extreme than attempting to produce sunlight throughout our city streets during the darkest of nights, which is exactly what happened with the advent of a public street-lighting system in the cities of 16th-century Europe. This is an example of a materiality that was slowly divorced from the domestic interior space, and then even further removed from the external adornment of residences until it became the responsibility of the city infrastructure. Authorities in cities such as London and Paris initially issued requirements for domestic homes to identify themselves with a display of light on their exterior,[1] regulations that were later to become more specific so as to simultaneously provide sufficient light for the streets immediately outside the homes. In time, such lighting strategies were almost completely removed from their relationship with the exterior domestic envelope and instead existed as lanterns, as freestanding elements of the street infrastructure.[2]

The light was used to police and exert control over the public city streets, but doing so required a subjugation and manipulation of the light itself. The intensity and spacing of the light sources became important issues in the development of the new systems, which most likely initially appeared as chains of single lights before the use of lenses and reflectors transformed them into something closer to pools of light that flooded the streets.[3] Such gradient typologies of light, which included the edge conditions of their boundaries, would prove to be of critical importance, focusing the research and development of public lighting in ways that had consequences for how public space and movement were controlled. As light became divorced from the domestic interior, explorations in determining its quality, intensity and radius reinforced the need to augment its properties so that it could take on the responsibilities associated with it, including illuminating thresholds between the buildings and the lit streets, as well as providing security and ownership of the circulation created as the light was pooled and chained down the street. Thus a gradient condition

Vatnsmyri Urban Planning Competition

Reykjavik, Iceland, 2007

In much the same way that the existing thermal pools on the site mix ocean water with recycled heated water from geothermal resources to create a unique condition for swimming all year round, the project looks to use these same thermal resources to affect the local climatic conditions on land, including air temperature and soil temperature for vegetative growth. Each of the programmed landforms proposed around the site is tied to the others by a climatic 'wash' that extends the seasonal activities, controls winds and permits an extended period of usable time outdoors during the course of the year. The wash permeates the public parks yet extends beyond to surround and engage the new building masses so as to produce artificial microclimates, and also acts as a connecting tissue from the north to the south of the site, a connection more substantive than simply providing a spine or corridor.

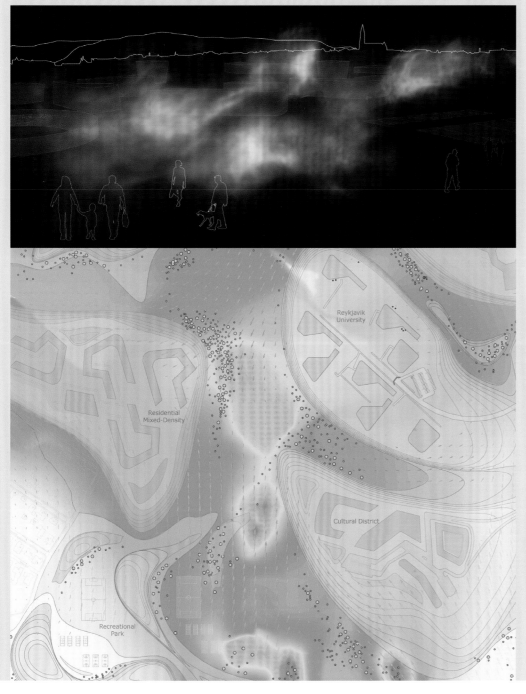

The Reykjavik proposal is an urban plan defined by gradient thresholds. Originating from the existing geothermal resources, the air, sculpted earth mounds and vegetative soil are warmed, creating variable microclimates for recreational activities, circulation and site organisation.

Estonian Academy of Arts

Tallinn, Estonia, 2008

WEATHERS' proposal for a new Estonian Academy of Arts (EAA) asserts its identity and position within Tallinn at both the level of the school's internal operations and that of its integration and connection with the city's need for public programmes, including parks, galleries and shops. This relationship between the internal operations of the EAA and its contribution to the city's infrastructure is a critical feature of the school's design.

The relationship between students and the city is mediated by a year-round public park. A series of Artificial Climatic Lungs located in six zones along the building connect the school above to the public park below. The park itself is located on top of the school's primary mechanical systems and workshop half a storey off the street, collecting and amplifying the building's captured energy to produce lush artificial gardens throughout Estonia's long winters. The zones also provide full-spectrum lighting to counteract the short daylight hours at this time of year. The building's light source for close to a third of the year comes not from the sky, but from the glass 'lungs' which form the true facade of the building and visually connect the student studios to the public on the streets below while maintaining a necessary security of space. As the lungs move up the building through three levels of studios, they also act as thermal collectors: as heat rises to the top towards the upper floors, it pools internally within the enclosed roof for external use by students as they enter from the floor above. These organisational devices are exposed to the external environment, but are nested internally in the building envelope and fed by the building's heat.

Model showing the Artificial Climatic Lungs located above the park, moving up through the floor plates of the academy.

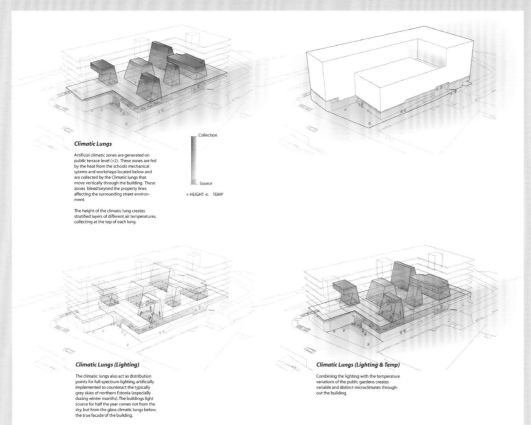

Climatic Lungs

Artificial climatic zones are generated on public terrace level (+2). These zones are fed by the heat from the schools mechanical sytems and workshops located below and are collected by the Climatic lungs that move vertically through the building. These zones bleed beyond the property lines affecting the surrounding street environment.

The height of the climatic lung creates stratified layers of different air temperatures, collecting at the top of each lung.

Collection

Source

+ HEIGHT vs. TEMP

Climatic Lungs (Lighting)

The climatic lungs also act as distribution points for full-spectrum lighting, artificially implemented to counteract the typically grey skies of northern Estonia (especially during winter months). The buildings light source for half the year comes not from the sky, but from the glass climatic lungs below; the true facade of the building.

Climatic Lungs (Lighting & Temp)

Combining the lighting with the temperature variations of the public gardens creates variable and distinct microclimates throughout the building.

Organisational strategies throughout the site.

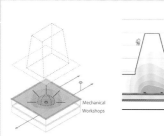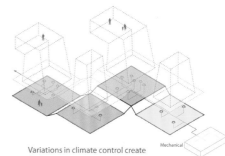

Point sources allow climate control.

Upper levels utilise climate zones below. Lighting from below illuminates studio spaces above.

Variations in climate control create distinct zones.

View along the street looking onto the public park with the academy programmes above. The public city park is located above the school's primary mechanical systems and workshop, collecting and amplifying the area's captured energy to produce lush artificial gardens throughout Estonia's long winters.

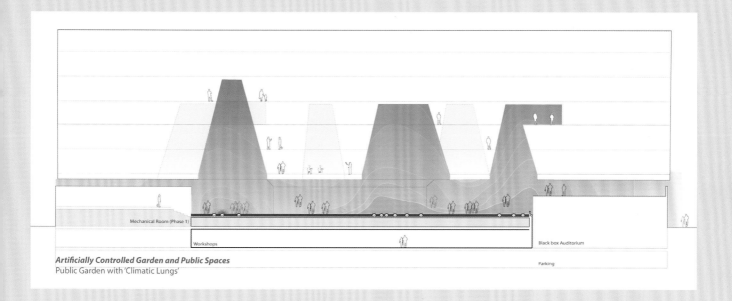

Mechanical Room (Phase 1)

Workshops

Black box Auditorium

Parking

Artificially Controlled Garden and Public Spaces
Public Garden with 'Climatic Lungs'

Tamula Lakeside Planning

Võru, Estonia, 2008

Urban planning is generally associated with a process of programme allocation and siting. The programme volumes are then tethered to a particular infrastructure that provides access and resources. Such planning strategies can often be one-dimensional in their approach, resulting in a rigid and isolating organisation of space. Existing regional climates and local site microclimates are rarely operated upon, and only defended against. Yet they play a large role in a programme's use, acting as the determining factor in the spatial allocation of programmatic activity over the course of a year. These climatic materialities (artificial or otherwise) have proved to be just as important in a site's organisation as the structures built to house specific programmes and activities. They can also play equally essential roles in larger spatial and urban planning. Many – if not most – activities at the urban scale, such as recreational or commercial activities and traffic circulation through a town or city, are linked to the exterior environment, thus climatic factors are a crucial component of any development plan. The Tamula Lakeside proposal is an attempt to meet the programme and activity needs of the site while simultaneously addressing seasonal planning: an attempt to consider how activities change throughout the course of the year while also creating opportunities for their artificial extension. These are neither landscapes nor building strategies, but climatic strategies.

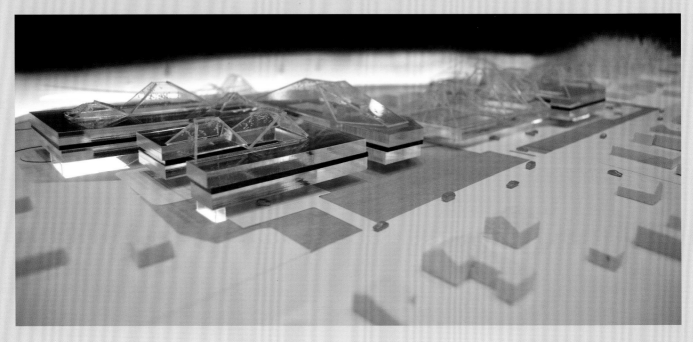

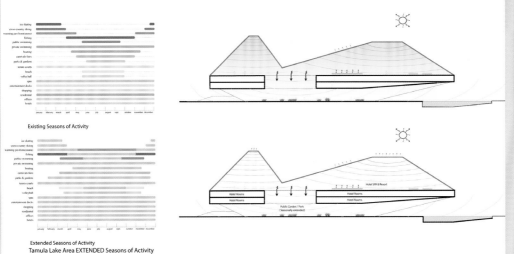

Existing Seasons of Activity

Extended Seasons of Activity
Tamula Lake Area EXTENDED Seasons of Activity

above: View of the proposal showing the building masses lifted from the ground for energy sources collected in the pyramids above to spill into the site and activities below.

left: Pyramidal shapes span the top floor of the building mass, capping the voids within the floor plates. These forms are made of various materials based on the programme activities below and serve to create and trap energy, which is translated as heat and light to produce the artificial climates below the voids. Such climate zones expand and contract in size and strength, growing to connect to other buildings and zones in the summer months and shrinking back into the building during the colder winter months.

Interior conditioned space
vs.
Exterior un-conditioned space

Pocket Parks
(Artifically - Conditioned)

Building lifted OFF Ground
Seasonal expansion below

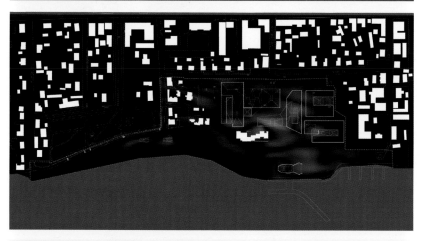

Seasonal Expansion

Summer Months

In the warmer summer months, climatic zones and gardens are at their most expanded state. These climatic zones of activity feed into each other as they mix with the surrounding environment.

Fall Months

As the fall and winter months begin, the zones are smaller and recess closer to the buildings. The energy and light that the pyramids produce facilate the gardens, pocket parks, and activities around them, radiating from below the buildings.

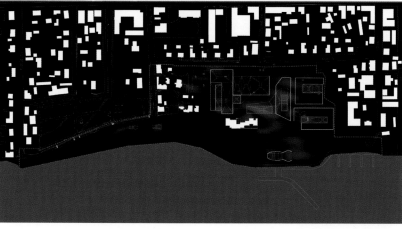

Winter Months

During the winter months when the natural light is sparse and the temperature has dropped, the pyramids and the pocket parks below are the main resources for alternate outdoor activities. These resources and opportunities also exist in the pyramids themselves with restaurants above the commercial space, hotel spa and the pavillion along the boardwalk.

Gradient climate zones are created on the ground floor of each of the buildings, growing and shrinking with the seasonal changes. These gradient parks shift in size and intensity, often spilling out and connecting with each other in milder seasons, while shrinking and acting as disparate entities in the more extreme winter months.

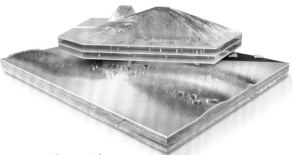

Commercial

summer day: The ground level of the complex provides a shaded, pleasant area to enjoy the park and watch the shopping activity above, with glimpses of the deck level which is bright with filtered sunlight.

winter night: All of the commercial activity has retreated away from the snow, within the building enclosure, where artificial light and heat generated from the building and activity has created a warm, semi-enclosed area around the pocket park.

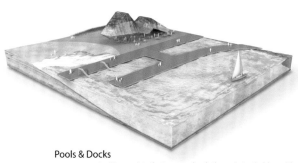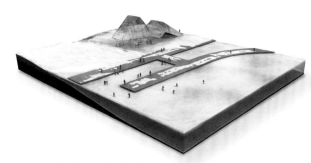

Pools & Docks

summer day: There are lots of swimmers and sunbathers enjoying the lake, and the boat dock area is active with small sailboats coming and going. The dockside structure provides a shady place to change and have a drink by the lake.

winter day: The semi-enclosed pools have frozen over, and the docks serve as launching platforms for visitors ice-skating and ice-fishing. The theater structure stays warm and protected, providing a warm and welcoming place to escape the cool weather and watch the ice-skaters in comfort.

Hotel / Spa

summer day: Hotel guests stroll to the beach nearby or swim in the shaded pool on the groundfloor, while spa visitors enjoy the facilities and views from the terrace above.

winter day: Warmth from the building and spa facility is enclosed by the canopies above, creating a comfortable artificial climatic zone within the hotel and spa facility, and activity around the building is pulled closer into the warmer core..

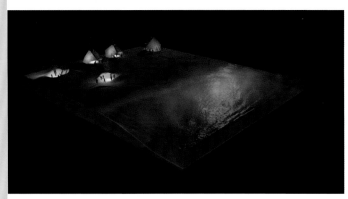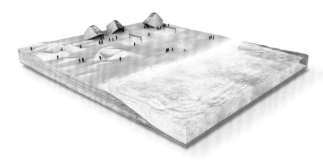

Beach / Waterfront

fall night: It is not snowing yet, but the weather is cold and most of the beach activity is centered around the fire pit and warming stones, creating pockets of warmth and light along the shore.

summer day: The beach will be at its busiest, with lots of sunbathers and swimmers. Shade is offered by smaller canopies, which cover outdoor seating and dining areas.

The primary focus of the project is an organisational system that is not only variable and flexible, but which is based on an 'expansion' of the existing seasons which are the main determinates of exterior activity and urban planning. The expansion of such activities, which are bound by environmental constraints such as temperature, precipitation and season shifts in daylight hours, is achieved with local climatic manipulations that harness the available energy produced by the glazed pyramid shapes of each building mass, creating expanded and alternate seasons and new programme overlaps.

coupled with a material was given a degree of responsibility beyond that of merely providing comfort.

Architects treat materials existing beyond the external envelope as a given context that the building must associate with or mediate against, and thus develop elaborate envelopes and strategies that attempt to temper exposure to the exterior environment. Biological analogies and contrasts are abundant in architecture, but seldom do architects think about the climate of the places that support the biological entities that are sampled for form, colour or shape as an actionable medium. It would be better to design this climatic context rather than concentrate all our resources on the objects and infrastructure we believe we must position within it. The focus appears to be on the air bubbles that float within a liquid; why don't we seek to engage the liquid as a medium for design itself? Rarely do designers question their role sufficiently to engage and redesign the environmental context.

The relationship of architecture to the context beyond its surface perimeter is one of confronting an omnipresent materiality that not only engulfs the building but permeates it as well. History gives a wide range of examples showing how architects and their design strategies have approached this surrounding context, ranging from the hermetically sealed interiorities of Le Corbusier's Cité de Refuge to the more romantic views of such architects as Frank Lloyd Wright or Richard Neutra whose residential projects sought a therapeutic link between the individual and what existed beyond the walls of architecture, each essentially assuming an ideal and constant condition of nature.[4] The underlying belief in each of these cases is that nature is somehow static. Nature today is clearly no longer outside human action, having become something 'carefully managed, skillfully staged, artificially maintained'.[5] Instead it is now a question of how far we can and will engage a spectrum of materiality that encompasses the parameters of nature itself, including its climates. Is it deceptive to even refer to an outside that is opposite to the interior? 'There is no outside: outside is another inside with another climate control, another thermostat, and another air-conditioning system.'[6] The question is, will we begin to act upon it directly, engaging it as a materiality or a design opportunity, or will it act on us only indirectly as a second-hand and third-hand repercussion?

The urban heat-island trend alone points to the extent that we are affecting our local climates and inadvertently creating microclimates all around us. With the genie out of the bottle, we are left to decide whether to let such augmentations continue as by-products of other primary actions or begin to operate upon these materialities and conditions first-hand, including them in design decisions.

It is often difficult to avoid the collusion that prevails between our artificially conditioned interior spaces and the surfaces and lines we use to represent the distinction between conditioned and unconditioned space. As our cities and megalopolises get larger, and we seek to understand and re-evaluate our place as architects in their formation – with cities either incrementally lurching forward or practically popping up overnight from previously unpopulated deserts of seeming nothingness – this simple dichotomy grows even more pervasive. Cities continue to expand and grow in complexity; as we have seen in the Middle East, they can grow in a very short time to proportions that should have taken decades to attain.

The design of climatic contexts seems more viable when looking to mechanisms of organisation that these newer city creations can only achieve by replicating centuries-old examples. History can point us to numerous architectural 'weather control' strategies, including Buckminster Fuller's Dome over Manhattan Island, but what we seek here is not the culling of recognisable climates for control to achieve preconceived notions of comfort associated with existing lifestyles, much as we would in climate-controlled interiors. We seek instead to produce and manipulate artificial conditions that will carry with them responsibilities (and likely prove to be subversive and ripe with repercussions) as we mutate, bastardise and reappropriate them as design materials for our organisational as well as aesthetic needs. This is not a question of controlling climatic conditions simply to meet predefined and understood contexts – longer seasons, transplanted microclimates or efficiency. This is a focus on how these very same climatic variables can become design materials with responsibilities thrust upon them that will inform and affect spatial organisation, something that requires environments currently not associated with existing climatic conditions. ⚙

Notes
1. Wolfgang Schivelbusch, 'Nightfall fear in the street', in Mirko Zardini, *Sense of the City: An Alternate Approach to Urbanism*, Canadian Centre for Architecture (Montreal), 2005, p 66.
2. Ibid.
3. Ibid, p 71.
4. Sylvia Lavin, *Form Follows Libido: Architecture and Richard Neutra in a Psychoanalytic Culture*, MIT Press (Cambridge, MA), 2004.
5. Bruno Latour, 'A Cautious Prometha? A Few Steps Toward a Philosophy of Design (with Special Attention to Peter Sloterdijk)'. Keynote lecture for the 'Networks of Design' meeting of the Design History Society, Falmouth, Cornwall, 3 September 2008, p 10.
6. Ibid, p 7.

OVERLOOKED THE DAY

The Work of Pierre Huyghe

BEFORE

Guest-editor <mark>Sean Lally</mark> describes two projects by artist Pierre Huyghe that use the materials and strategies of stage design – lighting, sound, fog and other atmospheric effects – and introduce them into everyday contexts. This effectively blurs the real with the fictional and calls us to question our own sense of reality.

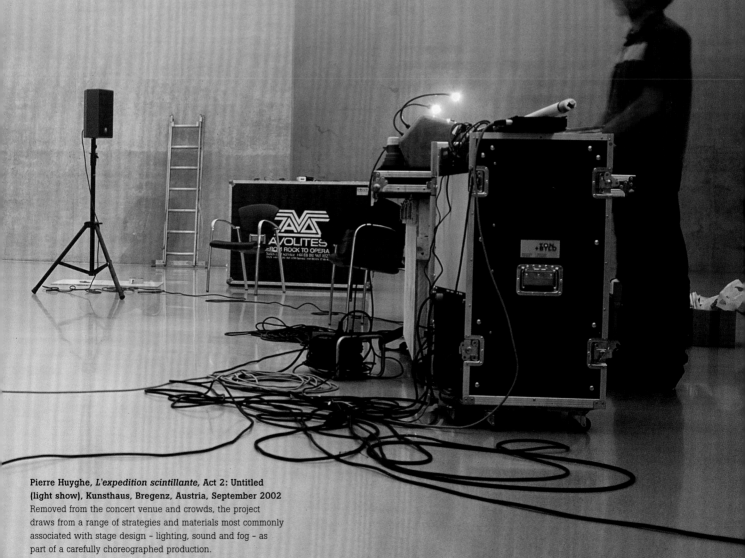

Pierre Huyghe, *L'expedition scintillante*, Act 2: Untitled (light show), Kunsthaus, Bregenz, Austria, September 2002
Removed from the concert venue and crowds, the project draws from a range of strategies and materials most commonly associated with stage design – lighting, sound and fog – as part of a carefully choreographed production.

Pierre Huyghe, *L'expedition scintillante*, Act 2: Untitled (light show), Kunsthaus, Bregenz, Austria, September 2002
Exhibition view, *L'expedition scintillante, a musical.*

The work of Pierre Huyghe blurs the distinction between what is reality and what is fiction, revealing the experiences he constructs to be as plausible as anything we would encounter in daily life. And though the projects often appear to be somewhat playful, they address significant social issues and reflect a communal yearning for experience and action in a manner that is just off-centre from simple utopianism.[1] The projects presented here are a small selection from a body of work that draws from a range of strategies and materials most commonly associated with stage design – lighting, sound, fog and other such means of atmospheric theatrics – and transplants them, along with the stories that accompany them, far from the security of the stage, instead embedding them into the environments we live in.

A Journey that Wasn't is a film by Huyghe based on a month-long expedition to Antarctica that the artist undertook with several companions. The journey was a search for a nameless island believed to have appeared out of the changing seascape; as the polar icecaps have begun to thaw at a rather unprecedented rate, uncharted landmasses are being revealed, offering new opportunities for the discovery of unusual ecosystems and previously unseen fauna. Specifically, the expedition to the island was a quest to encounter a solitary creature – an albino penguin – born from these new conditions.[2] Experimental equipment was developed in an attempt to make contact with the penguin by translating the physical shapes of the island into sound, resulting in noises that were not unlike the notes made by other animals native to the surrounding habitats.[3] These efforts centred on one simple objective: to attract the elusive creature. The quest was then re-created in Central Park, severing the mission from its original site and transplanting it into an entirely new reality. The team here attempted to rebuild the environmental conditions they experienced during their journey, such as the ice, light and visual qualities unique to the Antarctic island. Both the experiential construction and its urban reconstruction were documented for the final film.

Pierre Huyghe, *A Journey that Wasn't*, 2005
The film documents an expedition to encounter a solitary
creature – an albino penguin – born from the changing seascape
as the polar icecaps have begun to thaw. Experimental
equipment was developed in an attempt to make contact with
the penguin by translating the physical shapes of the island into
sound. Super 16 mm film and HD, video transferred to HD video,
colour, sound, 21 minutes 41 seconds.

Huyghe's film is based on a month-long expedition to
Antarctica. The journey was then re-created in Central
Park, severing the mission from its original site and
transplanting it into an entirely new reality. The team here
attempted to rebuild the environmental conditions they
experienced during their expedition, such as the ice, light
and visual qualities unique to the Antarctic island.

The theatre's organisation logics of
circulation and seating, and the relationship
of the audience to the stage, are erased as
the space for this 24-hour event is flooded
with vegetation, fog and lights.

As visitors enter into the space from the top of the hall they hear the music of a woman's voice drawing them into the vegetation, light and fog as they meander into a forest below.

Huyghe's *L'expedition scintillante* installation consists of three acts, of which the second, Act 2: Untitled (light show) is a re-orchestration of Erik Satie's *Trois Gymnopedies* (1988) by Claude Debussy. Removed from the concert venue and crowds, the experience is converted into a spectacle of coloured light and fog. Lighting devices are concealed in the plenum that seems to hover above its base, programmed to go off as part of a carefully choreographed production. Yet as the fog mingles with the lighting effects generated from above, the result is an experience made looser and more temporally fragmented as the music is no longer in sync with the visual spectacle.[4]

The projects here inhabit this in-between place. They are not quite fictional, yet they are more than a mere documentation of previous experience, giving the viewer little reason to believe such conditions and scenarios would not exist beyond the moment of viewing. Such design strategies place Huyghe's work away from any binary distinction of fictional versus real, and closer to something that does not exist today, yet hopefully we may find to be true tomorrow – or maybe, we just overlooked it the day before. △

Notes
1. See http://www.pbs.org/art21/artists/huyghe/index.html, accessed 30 November 2008.
2. See www.whitney.org/www/information/press/huyghe.pdf, accessed 30 November 2008.
3. Ibid.
4. Gloria Sutton and Pierre Huyghe, *Ecstasy: In and About Altered States*, organized by Paul Schimmel with Gloria Sutton, edited by Lisa Mark, MIT Press (Cambridge, MA), 2005, p 90.

Energy
Histories

David Gissen asks how architectural history might be reshaped by the new focus on energies, which will leave the conventions of the discipline redundant. Through three projects he investigates how the tools and preoccupations of history might be reinvented; whether it is through visualisations and conceptual reconstructions of a previously gas-guzzling age or through an atmospheric and climatic archive that replaces the primacy of the photographic archive.

David Gissen

Reconstruction of Midtown Manhattan *c* 1975

2002

The drawing engages with the long history of architectural
reconstruction, imagining the reconstruction of the corporate milieu
of the fully serviced buildings that first permeated Midtown
Manhattan in the 1960s. The intention is not to represent the
services themselves, but rather to visualise the overall urban effect
of the energy-age building. The image portrays what this milieu is as
an urban totality. It is in part a response to some of the images
within Robert Augustyn's and Paul Cohen's book *Manhattan in Maps*
(Rizzoli, 1997), in which the authors included efforts to map the
highly corporate Midtown sector of the city. The 'Bollmann Map', one
of the most graphically sophisticated representations of Midtown
Manhattan included in the book, is an extraordinary image; though it
shows the corporate terrain of Midtown well, it cannot capture either
how it feels to be in the very spaces of Midtown Manhattan or the
unique energy intensity that permeates this part of the city. For
example, between the mid-1960s and 1990s, Midtown Manhattan was
the world centre for intense indoor air-production; more indoor air
was 'manufactured' (so to speak) through the numerous fully
serviced buildings within this precinct than anywhere else in the
world. Reconstruction of Midtown Manhattan captures the immense
production of indoor air in these spaces – the scale of air
conditioning and its corresponding image of energy use. Here,
Midtown is imaged as indoor air and nothing else.

Reconstruction of Midtown Manhattan via an image
of its collective air-conditioned spaces.

In an age of architectural concentrations on energy, what will architectural history become? In an era in which the energy model and the fluid dynamic diagram compete with the photograph, how will architecture enter that space we term 'the archive'? How will the past that pre-exists the current energy obsession be revisualised and resurrected via a continued, yet expanded, emphasis on energy?

The three projects presented here begin to consider how energy as matter and media might impact a larger and new experimental approach to architectural history.

Within discussions of energy in the history of architecture, energy is often visualised through a charting of energy use or flow – via charts and diagrams – or as something in which the image of the building itself (its photograph) is a synecdoche.

Reconstruction of Midtown Manhattan, Urban Ice Core/Indoor Air Archive and Plume/Idling all examine energy as an expanded concept that might inform new historical analytical possibilities. They consider the very historical processes and image of history that a renewed focus on energy might engender, and further consider how this historiographic apparatus might beckon the production of a future work, specifically positioned to enter its particular logic. In other words, this historical work suggests as yet unrealised architectural efforts that, in turn, will be engaged by newly equipped historians.

These explorations of energy histories are forms of 'experimental history' – a historical analysis that simultaneously refers to a tradition of exploration while developing intrinsic norms in typically idiosyncratic ways that dismantle and reconceptualise those traditions.[1] This experimental work revives non-written forms of historical analysis – namely historical reconstructions and archives – reoriented towards contemporary interests. Both the reconstruction and the archive move through architectural history and theory – consider the fantastic reconstructions of Julien David Le Roy or the incredible image of the architectural archive developed by John Soane within his home and studio as but two of the myriad examples.[2] Both of these early modern projects explore the image of antiquity – a deep concern of architectural thought in early modernity. Though the contemporary efforts illustrated here are situated within the larger programmatic efforts represented by these two works, they also explore how reconstructions and archives might respond to emerging architectural agendas. This latter work also suggests how reconstructions and archives might refer to concerns in architecture yet to be given their due. The reconstruction and the archive are reactualised as powerful historiographic forms – the fantastical reconstruction, the fantastical archive – in a new experimental manner.

Within discussions of energy in the history of architecture, energy is often visualised through a charting of energy use or flow – via charts and diagrams – or as something in which the image of the building itself (its photograph) is a synecdoche.[3] Consider on the one hand charts of energy use that rely either on vector diagrams or energy metrics (for example, ventilation diagrams and comfort charts) or the recurring image in architectural historical examinations of the mid-20th-century curtain-wall skyscraper, where a fixed, inoperable skin stands in for a larger reliance on energy. These non-textual forms of energy illustration (which first entered architectural history via the work of Reyner Banham)[4] have been useful in considering the history of energy in architecture. But neither the metric nor ventilation diagram nor the photograph of the sealed skin adequately convey the particular intersection of its intense

David Gissen

Urban Ice Core/Indoor Air Archive

2008

Urban Ice Core/Indoor Air Archive carries the reconstruction efforts from Reconstruction of Midtown Manhattan into an exploration of the archive. It considers how this particular environment might be archived, both in Midtown and more broadly. This appears to be an important question as architects such as Philippe Rahm and WEATHERS increasingly experiment in their buildings with the production of new forms of indoor atmospheres in response to energy as a material and discursive form. While this work presents exciting new possibilities for producing new energy flows registered in air, neither the photograph nor the drawing suffice as means of 'storing' such buildings as historical artefacts. The specific content of the air of the interiors of the past is lost to us (its biophysical make-up gone); however, the Urban Ice Core/Indoor Air Archive is a fantasy archive for the retrieval of future data related to the types of manufactured atmospheres that now permeate indoor airscapes such as those of Midtown Manhattan and the work of selected contemporary architects. A speculative proposal, it imagines using current tools to study the air of the past, but wiring them in reverse. It appropriates the very archive that charts the collective, human impacts of energy use stored in air – the US ice-core project in Colorado – to archive the air within buildings. Samples of the air inside buildings are collected, injected into water and stored in tubes of ice, just like core samples from the North Pole or Antarctica. The project is intended as an agitation and reflection – a commentary on the work of contemporary architects interested in energy flow and its seeming resistance to traditional archival destinations.

Proposed archival techniques for archiving indoor air in buildings, appropriated from techniques used by scientists to study the Arctic and Antarctic.

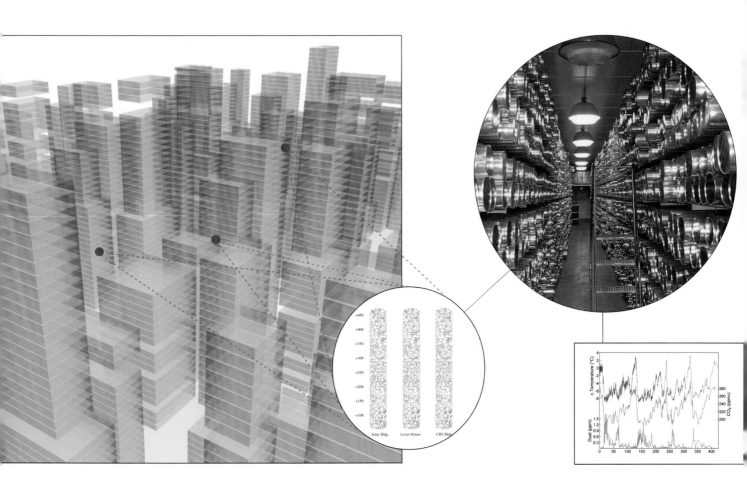

David Gissen

Plume/Idling

2008

Plume/Idling returns to the issue of architectural reconstruction. It entails a conceptual reconstruction of the exhaust plumes from the idling buses that once existed within a bus shed designed by Walter Netsch of Skidmore, Owings & Merrill (SOM) in San Francisco in 1951; the building now houses the California College of the Arts. The experience of energy in architecture is often through the environment that is produced for comfort or for specific forms of labour. However, the experience of energy often involves less pleasant, often odious substances – namely the by-products of energy produced by combustion. The reconstructed image of a historical architecture invariably eliminates these latter forms of energy flow. For example, in photographs of important historical buildings in Chicago at the turn of the 20th century, the skies are often filtered or fixed to minimise the city's often dense soot and smog, and the emissions of soot from the buildings themselves are eliminated in historical records. Certainly the published images of the original SOM bus shed lacked any sense of the noxious exhaust that moved through San Francisco at the time. The reconstruction of the plume not only forces a consideration of the particular form of materialised energy that once existed in this space; it also enables us to reflect on its relationship to the current comforting indoor environment of the school and the forms of production that bring it into being. In 'reconstructing' the plume, existing smoky emissions from a neighbouring coal-fired energy plant are filmed and projected onto the floor of the former bus shed.

character – the fleeting sense of temperature and sensation – within a more extensive framework that predominantly defines architecture. Most significantly, such images, which became the dominant historical representations of energy, were incapable of conveying what energy felt like, or the scale of energy as a form of matter in particular space-times. The energy-intensive interiors of the immediate past were spaces in which goose bumps and new chemical odours intermingled in vast zones of atmospheric production – zones that encompassed millions of cubic feet throughout corporate sectors of cities. Additionally, most historical analyses of architectural energy-use often miss all the other myriad forms of energy consumption that swirl around the architectural milieu. The energy-intensive city was one in which energy was pumped into buildings, but it was also a place expressed in plumes of exhaust and soot released from automobiles and power plants.

Considering the above methodological and historical concerns, how can energy be brought experimentally into that set of practices we label 'architectural history'? How can we both reconstruct the idea of energy that moves through aspects of postwar architectural history and archive our current energy-intensive interiors? One area considered in earlier work is indoor air – a substance that is both the product of architectural energy and a barometer of its effects. But air also needs to be considered more broadly as that sphere in which the by-products of energy – hydrocarbons, carbon dioxide, odours, smoke – are registered. Through various historical reconstructions and considerations of archives the three projects here arrive at images of air that are at the same time images of energy. They are by no means the only examples of how explorations of energy might involve experimentations in architectural history, but they do suggest how a reconsideration of energy and a reconsideration of history might coexist. **ᗡ**

Film and video animation reconstruction of an exhaust plume from one of the buses once housed in a Skidmore, Owings & Merrill bus shed in San Francisco.

Notes
1. I am grateful to my colleague Federico Windhausen, a historian of experimental film, for this definition of experimentation. For more on experimental history in social history see Daniel S Milo and Alain Boureau (eds), *Alter Histoire: Essais d'histoire experimentale*, Les Belles Lettres (Paris), 1991, and Daniel Milo, 'Towards an Experimental History of Gay Science', *Strategies*, No 4/5, 1991. See also the collection of essays edited by Robert A Rosenstone in *Rethinking History* 5:3, 2001, and Martha Hodes, 'Experimental History in the Classroom', *Perspectives: The News Magazine of the American Historical Association* 45, May 2007, pp 38–40.
2. See Julien David Le Roy, *The Ruins of the Most Beautiful Monuments of Greece*, Getty Publications (Los Angeles), 2003.
3. An excellent example of this is Reyner Banham, *The Architecture of the Well-Tempered Environment*, University of Chicago Press (Chicago, IL), 1969. Banham's imaging strategy is repeated in any number of environmentalist histories of architecture. For social histories of indoor air see Gail Cooper, *Air Conditioning America*, Johns Hopkins University Press (Baltimore, MD), 1998, and Michelle Murphy, *Sick Building Syndrome and the Problem of Uncertainty*, Duke University Press (Durham, NC), 2005. For a geo-architectural approach see David Gissen, 'The Architectural Production of Nature, Dendur/New York', *Grey Room*, No 34, 2009.
4. An exception to the Banhamite image of energy can be found in Luis Fernandez Galiano, *Fire and Memory: On Architecture and Energy*, MIT Press (Cambridge, MA), 2000, where the author explores energy as a transhistorical abstraction from Vitruvius to contemporary environmentalism.

Energy Forms

What impact does an energy-driven architecture have on form?
Cristina Díaz Moreno and Efrén García Grinda of AMID (Cero9)
outline their formulation of a new system for architecture that
is founded on a spatial understanding of thermodynamic
exchange and environmental systems and effects.

**AMID (Cero9), The Magic Mountain, Ecosystem Mask for
Ames Thermal Power Station, Ames, Iowa, 2002**
The project proposes a condition that refuses to exist in a false
dichotomy understood as either a natural or artificial system,
and instead seeks to construct another nature – a polluted,
altered nature, composed of landscapes manipulated and
acknowledged to be corrupted beyond repair.

If the aesthetics of the industrial production society era were based on simplicity, repetition or the assembly of additive systems, AMID (Cero9) proposes an architecture that is not concerned with its figure, but is instead characterised by a certain non-physical and non-visual presence: an architecture of energy in which its visible form is simply the materialisation of ambiences through mere energy management. During the postwar period, through the search for material and energy identification, the technological ideal of a minimum quantity of material was brusquely detached from the object's technological appearance. In this way, in the midst of the last century, geometrical systems and spatial configurations started to link together with the search for scientific efficiency. Without doubt this situation has opened the door to a new view of nature and to a new approach to form and configurations, all linked together – a view that could never be figurative, picturesque or just visual, but is driven by techniques and rigour operating at various scales.

AMID (Cero9) suggests moving from the architecture that in the postwar period worked with energy through organising matter in optimal configurations, in which the consumption of matter and energy was minimised through intensive research on form (Buckminster Fuller, Frei Otto), to systems in which the formal and material characteristics are driven by thermodynamic exchanges. The goal is a dynamic vision, with systems regulated by processes of energy exchange, with exteriors that dissipate, consume and capture energy: in short, complex organisations defined to manage energy through their formal characteristics, technical devices and material definition, all of which evolve over time. A building is no longer just the material form adopted by a particular and singular energy configuration, but a complex thermodynamic system that works through cold or heat, with or without order, with differences or homogeneity, and also evolves over time. A system that exchanges energy with the environment it is situated within. In this set of relationships and exchanges the inversion of the entropy arrow replaces both tectonic culture and visual predominance with a climatic approach. Instead of geometric composition, construction, structural thinking, surface design, parametric blankets or the proliferation of identical but different components, the aim is to define meteorological fields and landscapes at small scale.

In the case of a technical system that through the capturing or stimulation of energy induces spatial, environmental and visual effects, what we understand spatially becomes a set of perceptions linked to environmental effects generated through the management of various forms of energy. Architects become genuine specialists in special effects, linked now to a sense of

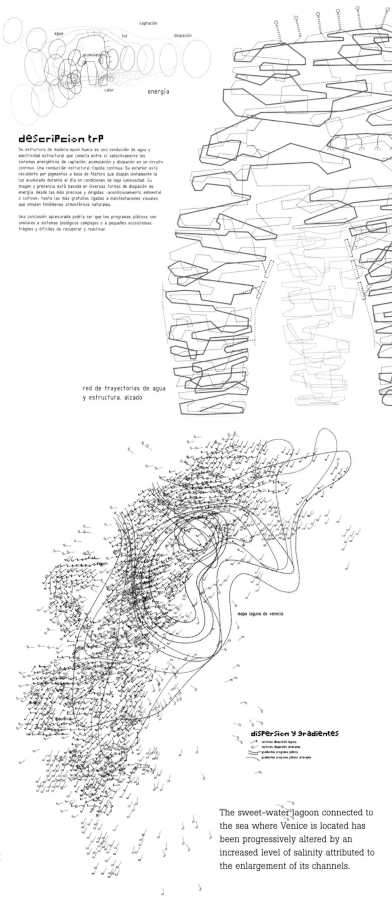

déScriPciⲟn trP

Su estructura de madera-epoxi hueca es una conducción de agua y electricidad estructural que conecta entre sí selectivamente los sistemas energéticos de captación, acumulación y disipación en un circuito continuo. Una conducción estructural líquida continua. Su exterior está recubierto por pigmentos a base de fósforo que disipan lentamente la luz acumulada durante el día en condiciones de baja luminosidad. Su imagen y presencia está basada en diversas formas de disipación de energía, desde las más precisas y dirigidas –acondicionamiento ambiental o cultivos– hasta las más gratuitas ligadas a manifestaciones visuales que simulan fenómenos atmosféricos naturales.

Una conclusión apresurada podría ser que los programas públicos son similares a sistemas biológicos complejos o a pequeños ecosistemas: frágiles y difíciles de recuperar y reactivar.

red de trayectorias de agua y estructura. alzado

mapa laguna de venecia

diSPerSion y gradienteS

vectores dispersión laguna
vectores dispersión alterados
gradientes programa público
gradientes programa público alterados

The sweet-water lagoon connected to the sea where Venice is located has been progressively altered by an increased level of salinity attributed to the enlargement of its channels.

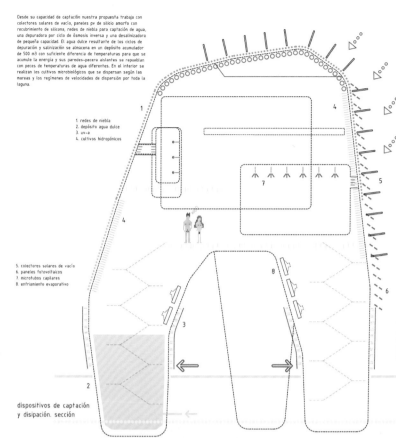

Desde su capacidad de captación nuestra propuesta trabaja con colectores solares de vacío, paneles pv de silicio amorfo con recubrimiento de silicona, redes de niebla para captación de agua, una depuradora por ciclo de ósmosis inversa y una desalinizadora de pequeña capacidad. El agua dulce resultante de los ciclos de depuración y salinización se almacena en un depósito acumulador de 500 m3 con suficiente diferencia de temperaturas para que se acumule la energía y sus paredes-pecera aislantes se repueblan con peces de temperaturas de agua diferentes. En el interior se realizan los cultivos microbiológicos que se dispersan según las mareas y los regímenes de velocidades de dispersión por toda la laguna.

1. redes de niebla
2. depósito agua dulce
3. uv-a
4. cultivos hidropónicos

5. colectores solares de vacío
6. paneles fotovoltaicos
7. microtubos capilares
8. enfriamiento evaporativo

dispositivos de captación
y disipación. sección

Estos objetos disipan energía de distintas formas: trabajan con el enfriamiento sensible, basado en la evaporación de agua y en su dispersión por medio de grandes ventiladores; poseen un sistema exterior de microtubos capilares de polietileno de 3 mm de espesor que conducen agua a temperaturas de trabajo moderadas (30 para calefacción y 18 para frío) para refrigeración y calefacción por efecto pared y una batería de rayos ultravioleta tipo A, con aporte local de infrarrojos para sensación invernal de confort térmico. En su interior contienen plantaciones hidropónicas de vegetales para consumo humano, sometidas a condiciones lumínicas controladas (cannabis sativa fundamentalmente)

AMID (Cero9), Forms of Energy, Venice Laguna, Venice Biennale of Architecture, 2002
The Forms of Energy project is a family of figures and mechanical systems referred to as TRPs. Each of these TRPs seeks to produce varied interior ambient conditions, conceived as generators of pleasure, evoking a sense of warmth, tactility or even a sense of shame for the occupant.

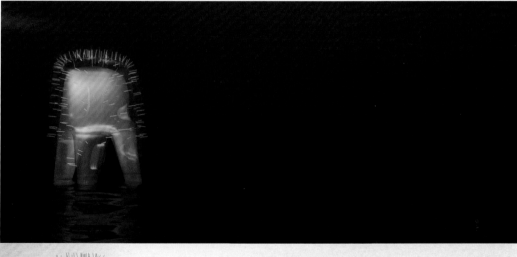

The project captures and harnesses the various forms of energy by-products associated with each of their environmental contexts to induce spatial, environmental and visual effects – a system in which space becomes a set of perceptions linked to these environmental effects.

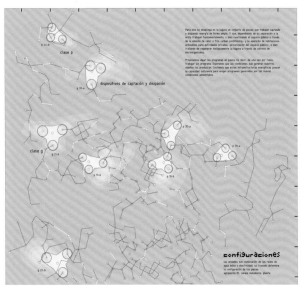

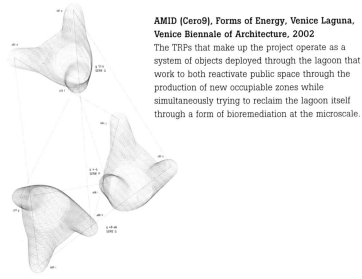

AMID (Cero9), Forms of Energy, Venice Laguna, Venice Biennale of Architecture, 2002
The TRPs that make up the project operate as a system of objects deployed through the lagoon that work to both reactivate public space through the production of new occupiable zones while simultaneously trying to reclaim the lagoon itself through a form of bioremediation at the microscale.

Forms of Energy is a network system of techniques deployed to capture and dissipate energy. Each part is defined by its ability and means for regulating processes of energy exchange with the environment it is located within. The project seeks to construct a new ecosystem for the lagoon as complex as a living biological network.

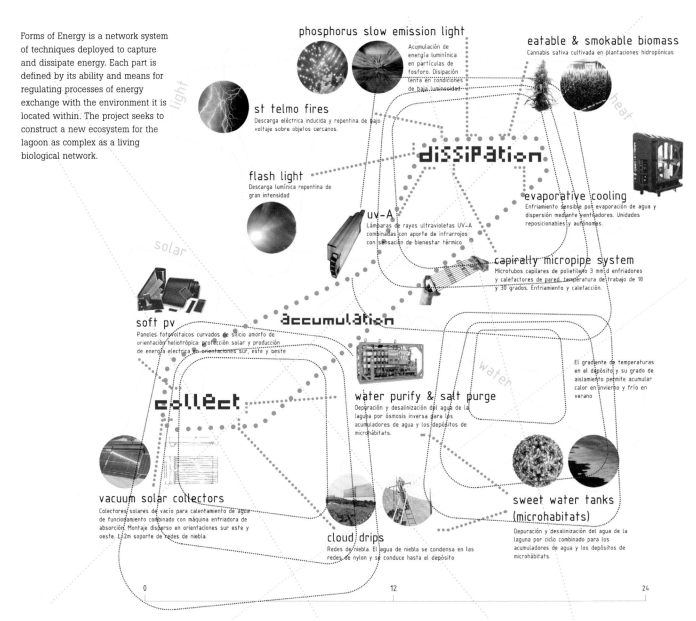

phosphorus slow emission light
Acumulación de energía lumínica en partículas de fósforo. Disipación lenta en condiciones de baja luminosidad.

eatable & smokable biomass
Cannabis sativa cultivada en plantaciones hidropónicas

st telmo fires
Descarga eléctrica inducida y repentina de bajo voltaje sobre objetos cercanos.

dissipation

flash light
Descarga lumínica repentina de gran intensidad

evaporative cooling
Enfriamiento sensible por evaporación de agua y dispersión mediante ventiladores. Unidades reposicionables y autónomas.

uv-A
Lámparas de rayos ultravioletas UV-A combinadas con aporte de infrarrojos con sensación de bienestar térmico

capirally micropipe system
Microtubos capilares de polietileno 3 mm con enfriadores y calefactores de pared. Temperatura de trabajo de 18 y 30 grados. Enfriamiento y calefacción.

accumulation

soft pv
Paneles fotovoltaicos curvados de silicio amorfo de orientación heliotrópica: protección solar y producción de energía eléctrica en orientaciones sur, este y oeste

El gradiente de temperaturas en el depósito y su grado de aislamiento permite acumular calor en invierno y frío en verano

collect

water purify & salt purge
Depuración y desalinización del agua de la laguna por ósmosis inversa para los acumuladores de agua y los depósitos de microhábitats.

vacuum solar collectors
Colectores solares de vacío para calentamiento de agua de funcionamiento combinado con máquina enfriadora de absorción. Montaje disperso en orientaciones sur este y oeste. L 2m soporte de redes de niebla.

cloud drips
Redes de niebla. El agua de niebla se condensa en las redes de nylon y se conduce hasta el depósito

sweet water tanks (microhabitats)
Depuración y desalinización del agua de la laguna por ciclo combinado para los acumuladores de agua y los depósitos de microhábitats.

0   12   24

AMID (Cero9), The Magic Mountain, Ecosystem Mask for Ames Thermal Power Station, Ames, Iowa, 2002
The living cladding that makes up the Magic Mountain project acts as a laboratory to experiment with, investigate and develop the genetic material of animal and plant species – a real-time laboratory of environmental conditions.

A disturbing silhouette in the urban scene, the Magic Mountain produces a second nature, not in contrast and juxtaposition to the man-made but as a complex interaction of human, natural and technological objects.

expanded perception and spatial organisation. And with its unstable equilibriums, its transitory states, its complex internal relationships and associated visual effects, architecture becomes an artificial atmospherics system on a reduced scale.

In recent years, the work of AMID (Cero9) has focused on systems that dissipate, consume and absorb energy dynamically in the shape of environmental systems. What is understood as space is therefore transformed into a set of perceptions linked to environmental effect generated by managing various forms of energy. Thus scarcely any visible environmental technology is required or produced, as the interest is shifted from the object towards that which is achieved. The focus moves from a system of relationships based on objects where their position, size and other formal characteristics generate figures, association and layout, towards a system based on the creation of reduced-scale and distributed environmental systems that are regulated by command sequences. It then becomes possible to work with the intensity of stimuli, with altered states and various levels of perception beyond that of the eye. For example, the sound volume of piano work composed by Morton Feldman is at times practically inaudible, requiring increased concentration and silence to engage with it. Here, the listener needs to amplify his or her capacity to hear and absorb their environment, which leads to an altered perceptive state they may otherwise not have reached. Working counter to Feldman's compositions, Brian Eno's ambient music requires much lower levels of attention and concentration. It is music that can be engaged with while we are doing several simultaneous tasks – it can be heard without listening to it. In this case, music is a tool that modulates and distorts our perceptions while at the same time working with different levels of sensorial privation and inducing new forms of attention.

Much of AMID (Cero9)'s work and research is driven by the possibility of activating public space through the insertion of small-scale mechanisms that could transform the ambient conditions within the city similar to that described by the music of Morton Feldman or Brian Eno, but with a range of materiality. In Venice, for example, the public space has been kidnapped by tourism. Nothing escapes from the market logic associated with this tourism, and the sterilising power of the image. AMID (Cero9) thus proposes enlarging the spectrum of technically modified conditions in the management of new public spaces. Forms of Energy (2002) introduces semipublic mechanisms that can be used for private purposes in hidden locations in the Venice Laguna to reactivate public spaces for inhabitants, inducing thermal, light and programmatic disturbances. Such 'urban conditioning' replaces the isotropy, homogeneity and universality of the modern 'well-tempered environment' with its climatic heterogeneity at the small, medium and large scale in the city, with thresholds, fields and perceptive gradients of temperature, light, colour, sound, smell or moisture. In doing so, Forms of Energy does not define figures. Instead the project constructs backgrounds which can become individual phenomena – blurring the figure, the image or even the architecture itself.

The emulation of the qualities of the thermal gradients and levels of light created by the project, whether natural or artificial, produces unexpected qualities that go beyond those of the original material.

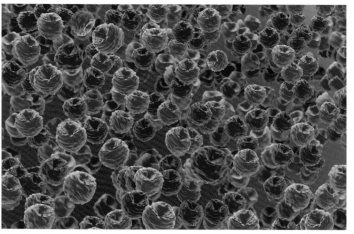

AMID (Cero9), The Magic Mountain, Ecosystem Mask for Ames Thermal Power Station, Ames, Iowa, 2002
Initial studies of colour patterns for the new skin are correlated to the colours of various rose species. The colour will vary through the years depending on the resistance and survival of each species. These changes will influence and inform the relationships and attributes of the various butterfly and bird species associated with the southward migratory route of the American continent within which the project is located.

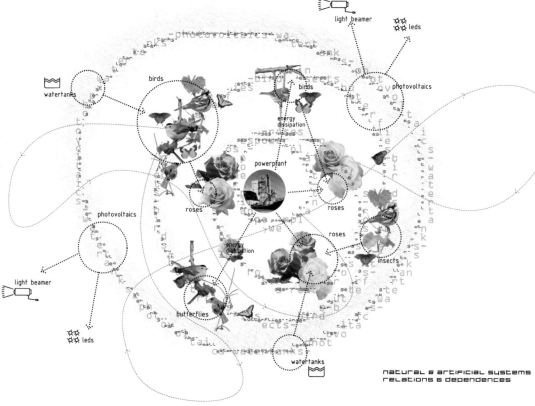

natural & artificial systems
relations & dependences

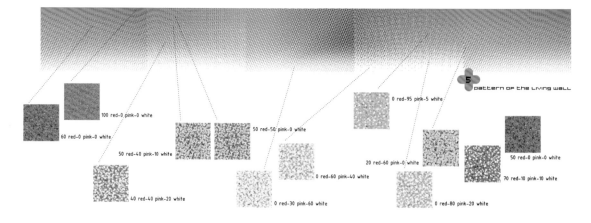

pattern of the living wall

100 red-0 pink-0 white

60 red-0 pink-0 white

50 red-40 pink-10 white

40 red-40 pink-20 white

50 red-50 pink-0 white

0 red-30 pink-60 white

0 red-60 pink-40 white

0 red-95 pink-5 white

20 red-60 pink-0 white

0 red-80 pink-20 white

70 red-10 pink-10 white

50 red-0 pink-0 white

A new skin wraps the existing building adding natural qualities and artificial material landscapes, developed and cultivated as a living organism.

Fake and synthetic offer further untapped opportunities; however, it is not just the visual conditions and origins of such materials that are interesting, but their performative conditions. Their artificiality and ornamental character are not negative states; they have the value of being in direct relationship with the effects they produce. However, only the effect, and not the essence, can be emulated. Synthetic, natural as well as artificial have been detached from what is usually called the true essence of things, and are now centred on how to produce effects. Thus we must redefine 'another nature', one in which it is irrelevant whether the living, material and climatic systems generated by it have natural or synthetic origins.

The Magic Mountain project was AMID (Cero9)'s response to an international competition for the refurbishment of an extremely large thermal power station running at full power right in the heart of the city of Ames in the state of Iowa. The architects proposed transforming the power station into a landscape within the city: a living mountain. This is achieved not by resorting to cosmetic treatment, to the erosive power of images and the kitsch assembly of local materials, but instead by challenging the established instruments and concepts of gardening, species breeding, architecture and the ecology of living.

Totally covered with a membrane of roses, honeysuckle and lights that fragment the volumes of the existing power station, the building's new skin wraps and adapts to the units at different heights, shrouding and unifying them with a silhouette and a single common material. Creeping above the highest parts of the building, the membrane transforms it into a vertical garden with living walls. The rose-bush creepers that form this vegetation crust are from the wealth of genetic material developed by Griffith J Buck (who was born and lived in Ames), who grew many species of roses adapted to the harsh continental climate of Iowa. The proposal also incorporates ancestral gardening techniques of genetic selection to create a

modern image in the uncomfortable presence of the power station. The living matter on the outer shell is planted in a grid of recycled polypropylene pallets, each measuring 1.5 x 3 metres (5 x 10 feet) and 7.6 centimetres (3 inches) thick. A structural box girder at the base contains the necessary subsoil for the plants to grow, and is attached mechanically to the reinforced-concrete walls of the station. A perimeter pathway between the shell and the walls facilitates pruning and upkeep of the plantings.

Ames sits directly on the southward migratory route of the American continent. As in a real mountain, the membrane is designed to attract the most important butterfly species in the northern US, at the same time transforming the power station into an open receptacle where various bird species can nest, attracted by the water tanks and insect populations in the vertical rose garden. The power station thus provides a resting place for migrating birds – an artificial alternative to the forests and wetlands that in recent years have disappeared from this area, and an ecosystem that is dependent on human interaction. Here, architecture and energy infrastructure are converted into living systems using bioengineering techniques to create a 'magic' mountain: a natural monument generated artificially.

New forms of social interaction, new design tools and manufacturing techniques to increase performative capabilities, and general concerns about nature and atmosphere as objects of design are completely transforming our material environments. Until recently it was convenient and comprehensible to divide our world into humans, objects and nature, attempting to categorise them in architecture through concepts such as utility, durability, optimisation or even ecological concerns. AMID (Cero9) instead sees the most effective and interesting opportunities not in the definition of built environments, landscapes or objects, but in the potential to technically transform through them the realm of interaction between humans and non-humans. The battlefield is that of the comprehensive and interdependent complex system of interaction between humans, nature and technological objects, the realm of the 'biotechnosocial', in which everything that is produced can be defined as a manifestation of all of these things at the same time. ∆

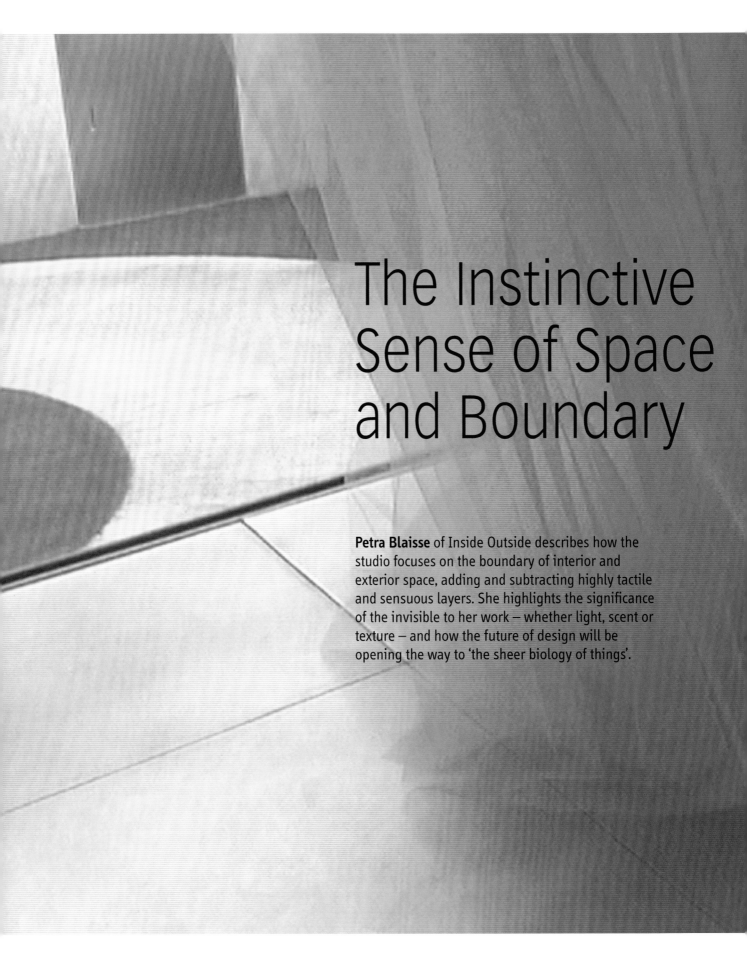

The Instinctive Sense of Space and Boundary

Petra Blaisse of Inside Outside describes how the studio focuses on the boundary of interior and exterior space, adding and subtracting highly tactile and sensuous layers. She highlights the significance of the invisible to her work – whether light, scent or texture – and how the future of design will be opening the way to 'the sheer biology of things'.

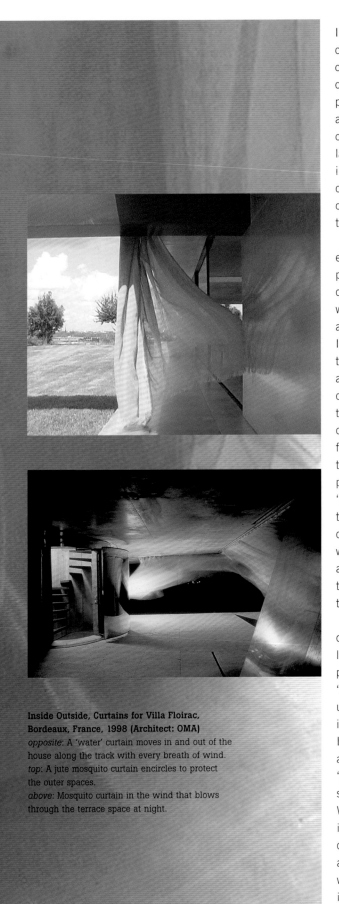

Inside Outside, Curtains for Villa Floirac,
Bordeaux, France, 1998 (Architect: OMA)
opposite: A 'water' curtain moves in and out of the
house along the track with every breath of wind.
top: A jute mosquito curtain encircles to protect
the outer spaces.
above: Mosquito curtain in the wind that blows
through the terrace space at night.

Inside Outside studio's interest in 'the boundary' and the
connection between inside and outside is not particularly
original; the essence of Modern architecture, after all, is based
on continuous space and seamless connection. There is a
preoccupation, a mutual influence and interpretation of interior
and exterior, even in classic (Western) architecture: the
organisation of the view through the window to the surrounding
landscape; the way that, inside, the image of landscape is depicted
in paintings, Gobelins, trompe l'oeils and on wallpaper and
curtains; and outside, the garden is organised as rooms with floral
carpets – offering a glimpse of 'another world' that isn't actually
there. And this is the basis from which the studio's work derives.

In architecture, the boundary is represented by the facade, the
entrance, the wall, the window, the door, the threshold, the
perimeter of a site or area, a building's footprint or volume. In
city planning it takes the form of roads, canals, hedges, gates,
walls, signs or built structures, or simply a dividing line of water
and land, prairie and forest, plain and mountain. Until recently,
Inside Outside have worked within the framework of visible,
tangible architectural conditions that have then been adapted by
adding or deducting layers in order to organise direction,
division, light, sound, heat and cold, at the same time addressing
the senses, triggering memory and reacting to time in two
directions.[1] This is usually achieved with interventions made of
flexible, pleated, stretched or folded soft materials (such as
textiles) of various degrees of absorbance or reflectivity; or with
plantings and different finishing materials. In short, with
'design'. Yet despite all our efforts as designers, our work is, in
the end, fundamentally dependent on phenomena beyond our
control and influenced by natural conditions such as draught,
wind, light, temperature, humidity levels and seasonal change,
and the requirements of the users. The designer's influence,
therefore, is minimal and only spans the short interval in which
the designs are drawn up and handed over.

Designers are sometimes invited by the marketing specialists
of large firms, and by developers, to introduce a 'design
language' that organises space, orchestrates traffic and the
pedestrian flow, and 'invites people in' by offering 'pleasure',
'shopping', 'lushness' and a form of 'well-being'. The language
used here is not only literal (in the form of signs, objects,
imagery, service areas, shops, restaurants, spas, gambling tables,
Internet centres, film and other visually titillating media), but is
also used in a more indirect manner to address our more
'primitive' layers of 'well-being': ambient music and synthetic
scents are thus added to the public space in which we exist.
When we feel 'well' and thus self-confident, we buy more and
internalise information more quickly, believing that what is
offered to us is the path to happiness and riches. Once our
alertness is tempered, we think and explore less as individuals;
we let go of our alertness, our own instinctive and acquired
insights, to be taken by the hand. From taxi, bus, train or plane
to shop to park to hotel lobby, bedroom or bathroom, we are

Inside Outside, Light-blocking curtain for Villa Haaksbergen, Haaksbergen, The Netherlands, 2008 (Architect: de Architecten Cie)
During daylight the pink of the velour lining shines through the grass print giving the green grass plane a smoldering purple glow.

Inside Outside, Curtain for Cinnabar Wharf Penthouse, London, 2002 (Architect: Busche Associates)
Like an intermediary screen between roof garden and penthouse, the translucent curtain extends the garden to the inside.

Sample of a voile scent curtain: the seam is composed of pockets filled with lavender buds, spreading scent while weighing down the lightweight curtain.

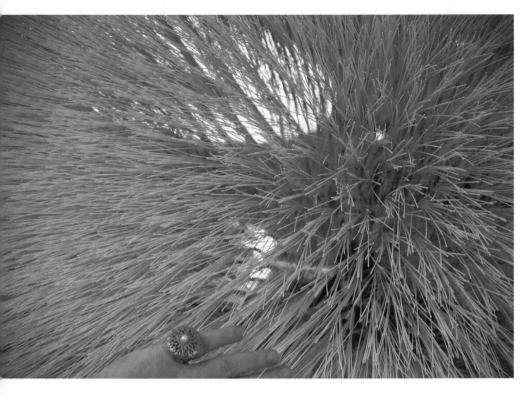

Inside Outside, Acoustic wall treatment for Mercedes Benz Museum, Stuttgart, Germany, 2006 (Architect: UN Studio)
Detail of brush panel for the acoustic treatment of a curved wall in the coffee shop. The long, thin hairs are inserted within wooden panels clad with reflective metal, creating the effect of continuous (borderless) space.

surrounded, steered and orchestrated by design; by one-liners that are easy to digest by all. Contradiction, friction and tension are out; clarity, simplicity and well-being are in. But no matter how strictly we try to control these environments, a primal level of memory continually exists within our minds. When something triggers this memory, our first reflex will be typical and immediate, because, like all living creatures, our first reactions to situations are developed in the first three years of our existence. For a fraction of a second – before our brain takes over – we will always react without thinking.

Ever since I was young, I have been conscious of the various warm or cold, light or dark climates in which we live, from the Mediterranean to the North Pole, enriched by the sounds of language, music and song, and taking in the local forms of dance, fashion, architecture and visual arts. Then there was my unwavering fascination with all forms of growth: animals large and small, and nature in general – its smells, its sounds, its vastness, the mixture of fear and consolation of the 'unknown'. I loved sleeping outdoors, wide awake, listening to the sounds and watching snails, night owls and bats by moon- or torchlight; climbing trees to find nests, seeds, webs, beehives; crouching to study ant hills, soil heaps, animal droppings, ponds and streams; watching documentaries for hours on end to discover the intricacies of everything that crawled, swam, ran, flew, burrowed, climbed or slid forward. I was fascinated by the colours and forms of all these creatures, their transformations, movements and stillness, the sounds that each species produced, the

shifts of tone, rhythm and frequency, and reading about their evolution through time. As designers we strive to engage these initial fascinations and pull them into our work, making them part of the worlds we construct.

These earliest memories are always present in the work Inside Outside creates. Reinventing the qualities of light, scent and texture, and choreographing the movement of object and viewer, either consciously or unconsciously, the work attempts to trigger that first reaction, that fraction of a second in which we are not in control and are not being controlled.

It has now become clear that it is necessary for us to reconsider our profession: to start from zero and reintroduce the invisible, the subconscious, the action-reaction: the sheer biology of things. If our interest in the procedures and methods of nature resettles, then why not introduce biology into our work and into architecture literally? Let's start regulating processes in a less obvious, visible way and begin shaping environments that will evolve into things unforeseen. ⚙

Note
1. 'in two directions' here refers to the fact that many soft materials start to degrade the moment they are employed, disintegrating until they are no more. On the other hand, gardens start to grow and live from the moment they are planted, taking about 50 to 100 years to realise the designer's intention.

Potential Futures

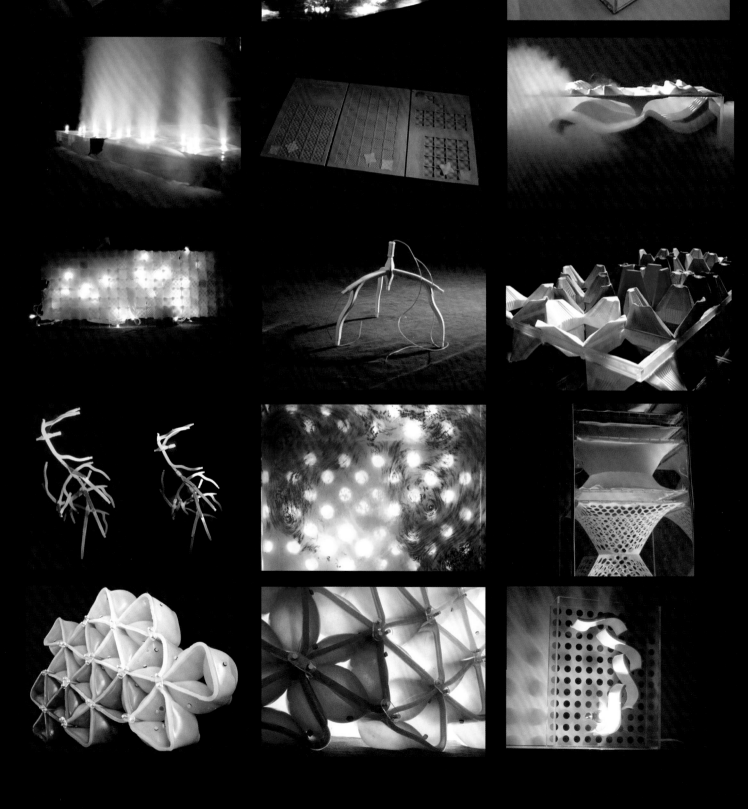

Mindful of the need to stimulate speculation and 'jump-start future endeavours', **Sean Lally** set his students at the Rice School of Architecture, in Houston, the task of questioning the notion of the boundary and investigating the realm of materiality associated with energy.

The main objective of the work from the Rice School of Architecture included here is not to question the role of process, nor to seek new and previously unseen representational techniques, nor outline a new manifesto to solve all others. Like the rays from a torch, the efforts are bound to bounce off a few things on their way to the objective across the room. The work is thus mindful of the methods and strategies that offer the resultant opportunities, but is always looking forward, continually glimpsing into countless potential futures – not only for evaluation, but for instigating new events. With such an approach, the projects act as facilitators to jump-start future endeavours that can be absorbed by additional associations in order to create opportunities and speculations that offer more than their own end product.

As designers question the role we are playing in the design of tomorrow, we acknowledge the power and proclivities of the tools and techniques we deploy and the information they quantify. And while the tool sets at our disposal seem to grow faster, stronger and more efficient every year, we need to remain mindful that our reliance on technology is often an excuse for a weak imagination. Our fascination and attention must extend beyond the protocols, tools and research to the potentialities and implications they provide. As designers, when our discussions fall into a defence of process and contemporaneity, we slip into a model of design practice that is self-referential and defined by protocols instead of opportunities. Design today is the search for these opportunities, not the scrutiny of the paths that get us there. The research and work at Rice is a generator of speculation and a reservoir for potentialities to be tapped when needed: not for manifestos and proclamations, but for inclinations and instincts as we tackle new projects still to come.

The work illustrated here is an attempt to question a rather fundamental and all too often ignored discussion in architectural education and design; what constitutes a physical boundary and edge in the spatial organisations architects create? The projects investigate a realm of materiality associated with energy as it pertains to defining and constructing physical boundaries in our built domain. As these are often oversimplified and pigeon-holed as either qualitative 'effects' or as part of a preconceived and efficient 'sustainable design', the projects address these 'material energies', which in themselves are rarely heralded as an opportunity for design innovation, with broader spatial and organisational implications in the foreground. Such innovation in design for local – as well as urban and regional – environments is most fruitful not at the level of the structural engineer's attempts to design better walls, but when it seeks to investigate a broader spectrum of materiality when questioning something as fundamental as what constitutes a boundary when organising activity in architecture.

Because energy is addressed as a design material to be exploited during the design phase, the work inevitably crosses disciplines ranging from architecture and landscape architecture into issues encompassed in the broader domain of urban planning; the materials involved are not mutually exclusive to a building, a landscape or a city organisation. Many of the projects and study exercises operate as full-scale investigations, not only through software simulations, but by the deployment of physical prototypes and fabrication intended to show deviations in results between the software and the physical tests. The investigations question those materials at the architect's disposal that are useful in the quantifying and instrumentalising phases in the design process. The results indicate an approach that does not see research as a product in and of itself; rather, the investigation is only as important as where it leads to next. The work is less about being fully executable 'complete' projects and more about a strategy of design that seeks a 'proof of concept' – a verification of a strategy that shows a potential for its future project endeavours.

Each of the projects relies on its inherent role as a generator for future opportunities and speculations. They seek to increase the feedback between the choices designers make and the evaluation of the prospects of these choices as we sieve through options and entertain daydreams of the imagination. If what designers are looking for is an ability to heighten and amplify the feedback loop between the ideas they generate, our ability to test and gather information about its feasibility and potential for success or failure, then the discussion becomes one less about the methods deployed in design and more about the spatial and social implications such work provides and instigates. It is the attempt to increase the rate of return that increases designers' decision-making abilities and knowledge base in the pursuit of design innovation. We strive to maximise those 'eureka moments' during the design process that propel us forward and beyond our previously linear trajectory. The work is an act of instigation with friends and accomplices rather than a search for a captive audience to digest and reflect upon our tactics.

Overview of student work, studios and seminars, Rice School of Architecture, Instructor Sean Lally. From left to right: (Alexandre Acemyan, Rosalynn Lu, Glen Negretti), (Doug Shilo, Ali Naghdali, Tim Kunkel), (Brad Naeher, Glenn Negretti), (Joe Lim, Doug Shilo), (Joe Lim, Doug Shilo), (Brad Naeher, Glenn Negretti), (Joe Lim, Doug Shilo), (Federico Cavazos, Robert Crawford), (Eric Hughes, Matthew Geiger), (Federico Cavazos, Robert Crawford), (Doug Shilo, Ali Naghdali, Tim Kunkel), (David Alf, Alice Chai, Benjamin Pollak), (Susan Crowe, Melanie Pratt, Anton Sinkewich), (Andrew Corrigan, John Carr).

Andrew Corrigan and John Carr

Reykjavik Botanical Garden

Graduate Option Studio (Sean Lally), Rice School of Architecture, Houston, Texas, 2006–07

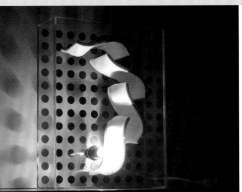
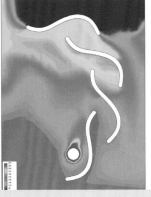
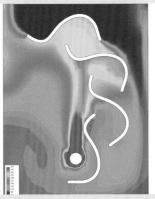
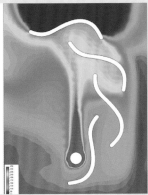

Reykjavik Botanical Garden is a hybrid system utilising Iceland's abundant geothermal energy resources to serve a series of convection loops that create microclimates for varied plant growth. Heat is taken directly from the ground and piped up across the landscape into a system of towers. The geothermal distribution system, operating at ground level, is exploited in order to warm the earth's surface and increase the plantable area. Zones of heat radiate out from the pipes, creating a new climate layer with variable conditions based on their number and proximity to each other. These exterior plantings are mostly native to Iceland, but the amplified environment allows a wider range of growth than would normally be possible, informing the role and opportunity of this particular botanical garden.

Visitors experience growth never before possible in Iceland, and travel through new climates throughout the site. Geothermal wells extract steam from volcanic fissures within the earth, which is directly pumped through pipes on the site. This network of interwoven pipes feeds 12 towers, each of which siphons off a portion of the available heat that rises within each tower and in turn draws in cooler air from outside in a convection loop. The towers contain a catalogued variety of plants from many of the world's climates. A system of intake tubes and chambers modulates the heat flow to hydroponic growing trays and research laboratories. The towers in the landscape are each slightly different, creating 12 distinct growing environments simply by rearranging the hydroponic trays and the air-intake systems within the towers.

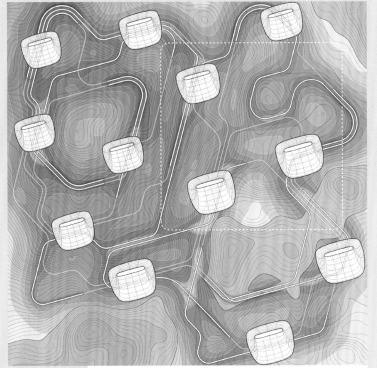

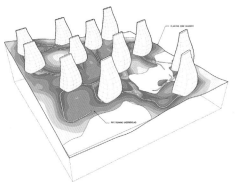

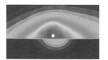

PIPE CONDITION: ABOVE GROUND

Above ground piping is efficient at heating the surrounding area but also blocks movement across the site. Used strategically, this type of condition can create demarcate habitation zones.

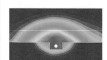

PIPE CONDITION: BELOW GROUND

Below ground piping obscures the processes at work but effectively stays out of the way.

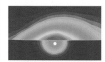

PIPE CONDITION: ENTRENCHED

Trenched piping is a compromise solution. Used together, these three conditions provide for a rich kit of parts with which to modulate the surface conditions.

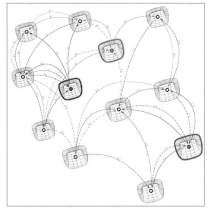

DISTRIBUTION NETWORK

Geothermal energy is supplied by wellheads in three towers. These three towers are primary nodes, labeled A, B, and C. Each of these nodes use three pipe loops, respectively, to deliver heat to the secondary nodes.

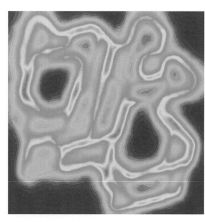

GEOTHERMAL ZONES

The distribution loops are configured to maximize the available planting area. Rather than simply running straight runs of pipe between nodes, the implemented system is designed to occupy the entire site. The combined geothermal zone map demonstrates the richness of climate variations across the landscape.

GEOTHERMAL POWER

Geothermal power refers to power generated from geothermal resources in the earth. Water within the earth is heated by volcanic lava, creating pockets of super heated water and steam. This is then piped out of the earth in either form, at which time it can either be used directly to heat buildings, or it can power turbines for the generation of electricity. There are three main methods for harnessing geothermal resources as diagramed at right.

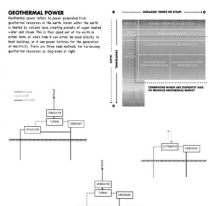

DISTRIBUTION NETWORK: NODE A

The entire distribution system consists of three overlapping sub-networks. Each of the three loops within each system is closed, bringing cooled water back to the source tower.

GEOTHERMAL ZONES: NODE A

The three pipe conditions (above ground, below ground, and entrenched) lead to a complex thermal situation. Though Node A serves the smallest number of other towers, this map displays the great range of varying climates possible.

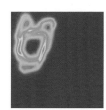

DISTRIBUTION NETWORK: NODE B

Network B is situated between the other two networks and helps to tie the system together.

GEOTHERMAL ZONES: NODE B

Trenched pipe conditions, supplemented by bridges for pass-over, allow for an unimpeded landscape but produce more heat than fully submerged pipes.

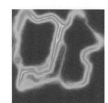

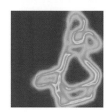

DISTRIBUTION NETWORK: NODE C

The network system is designed with redundancy in mind. The system can partially function with only one primary node online.

GEOTHERMAL ZONES: NODE C

Red areas in the thermal map display situations where two or more exposed pipes meet. These areas become dead areas in the planting diagram, as they are too hot to sustain plant life.

Heat can be exchanged through pipes using the countercurrent flow principle. When two pipes are run concurrently with a semi-permeable membrane, or a close proximity to exchange heat, the maximum exchange will be for both flows to reach equilibrium. But when the flows are run counterconcurrently, they can exchange nearly 100% of their heat. By keeping the heat exchange gradient constant across the transfer surface, maximum exchange can occur.

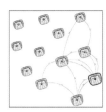

Curt Gambetta and Brian Shepherdson

Living in Coils

Graduate Option Studio (Sean Lally), Rice School of Architecture, Houston, Texas, 2007–08

What if a home was an air conditioner? This project proposes a model of living organised around the movement and humidity of air. Located in Houston, the map of humidity within the city recalls the contrasts of Giambattista Nolli's 1748 plan of Rome, though here the contrast is drawn between internalised, conditioned space and external atmosphere. Air conditioning and waterproofing of materials work to fortify the home against the intrusion of water vapour, creating a homogeneous environment of hard programmatic enclosures. This reinforces an organisation of living of which we wish to be critical, at both the scale of the unit and of the city. In this project, humidity is thought of as a generative force, rather than a nuisance, imagining an environment where the affective qualities of air movement and moisture content engender soft boundaries and unit cohabitation through air exchange.

In the conventional home environment, air is processed at a discrete and centralised point in order to achieve homogeneous qualities of smell, temperature and humidity that are distributed to distinct volumes of residential programme. The point-fed distribution of the conventional air-conditioning unit is here supplanted with a field of distributed air-processing units that comprise both floor and ceiling surfaces. The interior of the prototypical unit draws air across its cooled upper surfaces, removing water vapour through condensation and collecting it in channels. Fields of these units hover above vapour-producing activities, pulling air upwards and softly emitting it into the environment above. By modulating both the intensity of these fields and the volumetric sizes of atmosphere they work to define, patterns of domestic living are created. Self-interested cells of conditioned space become an ecology of conditions.

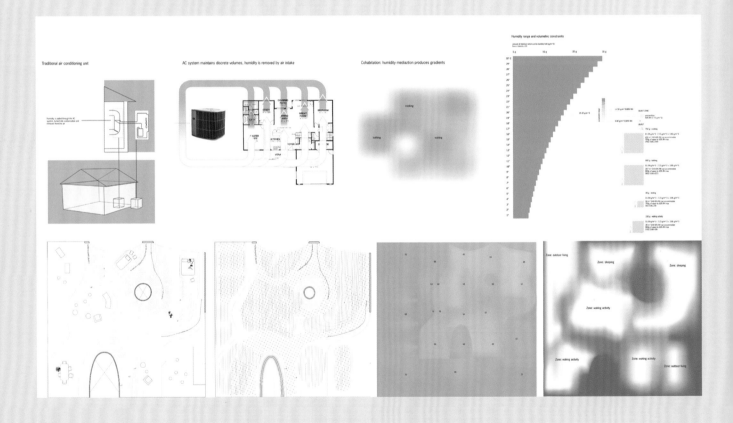

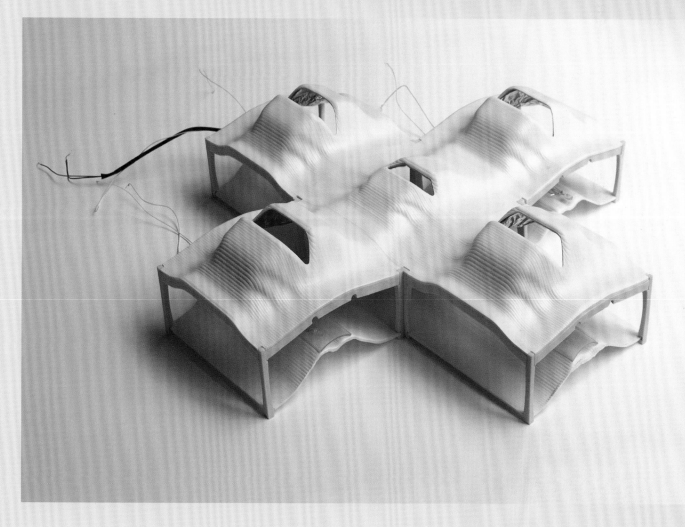

Ned Dodington and Brian Love

We Do Not Live in a Mono-Climatic World

Graduate Option Studio (Sean Lally), Rice School of Architecture, Houston, Texas, 2007–08

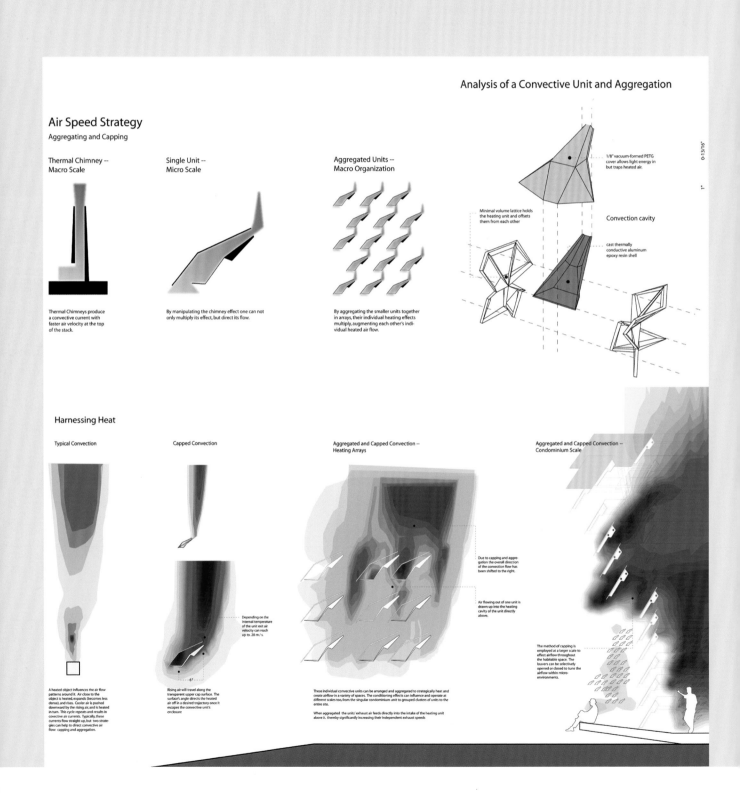

The project proposes a strategy for a domestic space embedded within our local environments, in this case within an urban-scale convective flow. Modelling software was used during the course of the studio to develop and test both the performance of discrete pods and the system as a whole. A combination of digital fabrication techniques was then used to prototype each pod at full scale. The pods are a combination of three parts: an aluminium-filled epoxy-resin base collects and radiates heat, and a vacuum-formed acrylic top captures and directs convective flow while these two pieces sit in a lattice structure for system-wide aggregation and control. Residential living is rewritten to become complicit with larger augmented macro-environmental conditions. Now in a seminomadic state, programme relocates within the building at different times of the day and year. Convection and air pressure become fully participant as materials for controlling, and celebrating a new way of life in the convective flow.

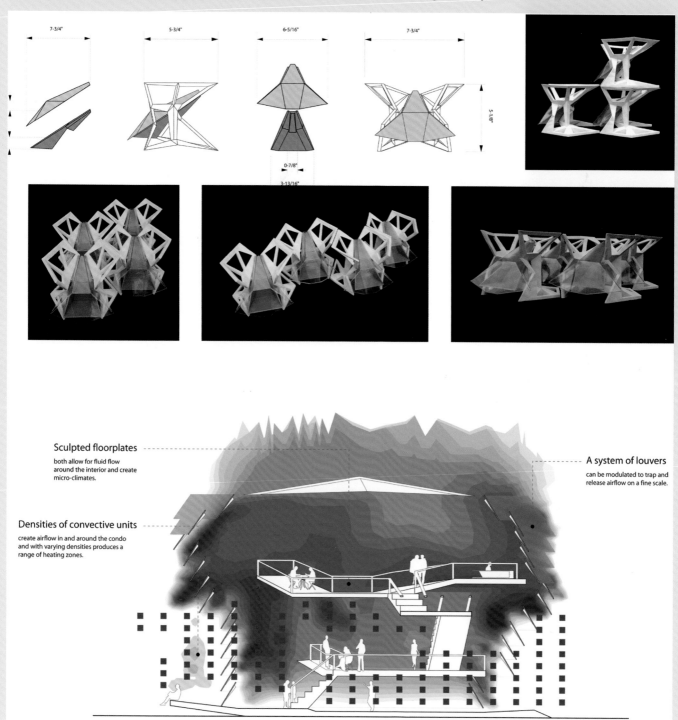

Sculpted floorplates
both allow for fluid flow around the interior and create micro-climates.

A system of louvers
can be modulated to trap and release airflow on a fine scale.

Densities of convective units
create airflow in and around the condo and with varying densities produces a range of heating zones.

Federico Cavazos and Robert Crawford

Ambiguous Etiologies

Vertical Option Studio (Sean Lally), Rice School of Architecture, Houston, Texas, 2006–07

Ambiguous Etiologies is a reconfigurable modular lattice system that minimises Wyoming's large temperature swings from summer to winter in order to create a year-round inhabitable outdoor space. The pavilion harnesses water, wind and snow to create a landscape of differentiated spatial zones. During the frigid winter months, the components' semiporous aggregations act as snow fences, slowing down drifting snow enough to accrue into moguls. These mounds, or 'fetches', of snow are calibrated to accumulate behind and in front of the fences to a size that is proportionally scaled to their human occupants. The hollow modules comprising the fences act in conjunction with the fetches to insulate space and reduce wind chill. Furthermore, nichrome, a heating metal alloy, is spliced into the modules' connections to warm the inhabitable spaces downwind. These space heaters, many buried within the mounds, are activated just before the hot summer months to melt the stored snow and ice into a series of pools upwind. Breezes blow over these pools cooling the pavilion while the fences now provide shade in the barren plains. The pavilion contemporaneously shapes its climate and is shaped by it.

The orchestration of these complex and inseparable spatio-temporal forces necessitated using digital and analogue feedback loops at the scale of the module and the pavilion. The loops tested the structural stability and electrical conductivity of modules, as well as the aerodynamics, heat output and insulating capacity of different component aggregations and their fetches. Growth of the various distributions' fetches was simulated with a digital script derived from government-funded snow fence research data, and the feedback from the different trials was constantly integrated into each other as well as the design of the module and its arrangement. This generative design process simultaneously affected, and was affected by, the aforementioned performance criteria.

The pavilion challenges the understanding of space as a 'discrete multiplicity', and approaches architecture as the dynamic distribution of intensive material properties: conductivity, ductility, density, temperature, pressure, velocity. Ambiguous Etiologies acknowledges architecture's full immersion in the flux of material energies, revealing the absurdity of dialectic categories such as the natural and the artificial, or the landscape and the building. It is an engine for the organisation of matter. ∆

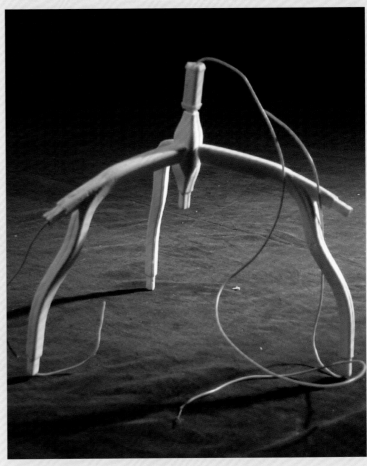

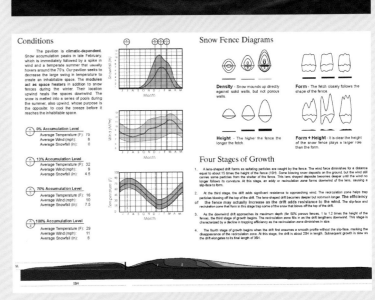

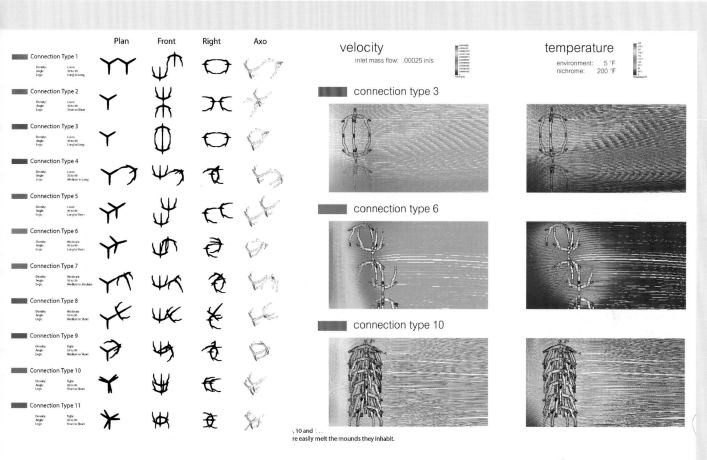

	Plan	Front	Right	Axo
Connection Type 1 Density: Loose Angle: 90 to 90 Legs: Long to Long				
Connection Type 2 Density: Loose Angle: 90 to 90 Legs: Short to Short				
Connection Type 3 Density: Loose Angle: 90 to 90 Legs: Long to Long				
Connection Type 4 Density: Loose Angle: 30 to 90 Legs: Medium to Long				
Connection Type 5 Density: Loose Angle: 90 to 90 Legs: Long to Short				
Connection Type 6 Density: Moderate Angle: 90 to 90 Legs: Long to Short				
Connection Type 7 Density: Moderate Angle: 30 to 30 Legs: Medium to Medium				
Connection Type 8 Density: Moderate Angle: 30 to 90 Legs: Medium to Short				
Connection Type 9 Density: Tight Angle: 30 to 90 Legs: Medium to Short				
Connection Type 10 Density: Tight Angle: 90 to 90 Legs: Short to Short				
Connection Type 11 Density: Tight Angle: 90 to 90 Legs: Short to Short				

velocity

inlet mass flow: .00025 in/s

temperature

environment: 5 °F
nichrome: 200 °F

connection type 3

connection type 6

connection type 10

, 10 and ` . . .
re easily melt the mounds they inhabit.

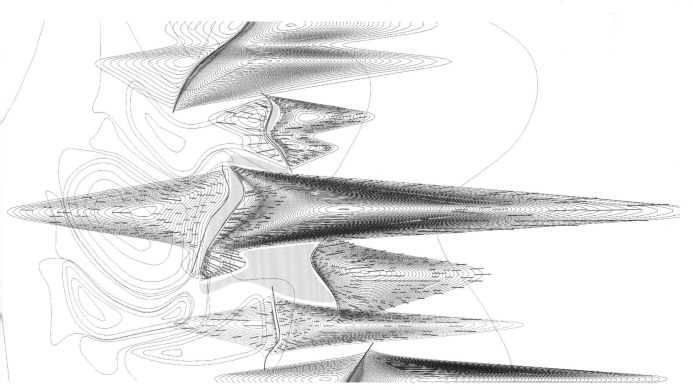

Contributors

Michelle Addington previously worked at NASA/Goddard Space Flight Center, where she developed structural data for composite materials and designed components for unmanned spacecraft, before spending a decade as a process design and power plant engineer as well as a manufacturing supervisor at DuPont. After studying architecture, she became an architectural associate at a firm based in Philadelphia. Her work includes the research of discrete systems and technology transfer, and she serves as an adviser on energy and sustainability for many organisations, including the Department of Energy and the American Institute of Architects. She co-authored (with Daniel Schodek) *Smart Materials and Technologies for the Architecture and Design Professions* (Architectural Press, 2004), and is currently an associate professor at the Yale School of Architecture.

Cristina Díaz Moreno and **Efrén García Grinda** started their Cero9 partnership, now known as AMID, in 1997. Located in Madrid, they have facilitated a real connection between professional practice, research and teaching. They have won more than 30 prizes in national and international architectural competitions, and their work has been featured at the Venice Biennale of Architecture (in 2000, 2002 and 2004) and the London Architecture Biennale (2006), as well as at the exhibitions 'Space for your Future' (MOT Tokyo, 2007–08), 'Invisible Architecture' (CCS, Paris, 2005) and at ArchiLab 2001. They have been associate professors of architecture at ETSAM and ESAYA (Madrid) since 1998, and were visiting professors at Cornell University in 2007.

Petra Blaisse began her career at the Stedelijk Museum in Amsterdam, in the Department of Applied Arts. From 1987 she worked as a freelance designer and won distinction for her installations of architectural work, in which the exhibited work was challenged more than displayed. Her focus gradually shifted to the use of textiles, light and finishes in interior space and, at the same time, to the design of gardens and landscapes. In 1991 she founded Inside Outside. The studio works in a multitude of creative areas, including textile, landscape and exhibition design. Since 1999 she has been inviting specialists from various disciplines to work with her, and the team currently consists of about 10 people of different nationalities.

Penelope Dean is Assistant Professor of Architecture at the University of Illinois in Chicago. She is an architect and writer and previously taught design and theory at OSU, the Bauhaus Dessau and the Rietveld Academy, Amsterdam. She was the editor of the Berlage Institute's journal *hunch* between 2003 and 2007, and has served as an editorial consultant for *Crib Sheets*, *Content*, and *KM3*. A registered architect in the Netherlands, she worked at the Dutch office MVRDV from 1998 to 2002. Her articles have been published in *Log*, *Trans*, *Archis*, *Architectural Record*, *hunch* and *Praxis*, and her ongoing research proposes how architecture might redirect the techniques of a generalised design field for its own uses.

David Gissen is an assistant professor in the departments of architecture and visual studies at the California College of the Arts. Current work includes the book *Subnatural Architecture* (Princeton Architectural Press, 2009) and the essay 'The Architectural Production of Nature, Dendur/New York' for the MIT Press journal *Grey Room*.

Pierre Huyghe attended the École Nationale Supérieure des Arts Décoratifs, Paris, from 1982 to 1985. Employing folly, leisure, adventure and celebration in creating art, his films, installations and public events range from a small town parade to a puppet theatre, from a model amusement park to an expedition to Antarctica. He lives and works in Paris and New York, and has had solo exhibitions throughout the world including at Tate Modern in London and the Modern Art Museum of Fort Worth, Texas (2004), the Solomon R Guggenheim Museum, New York (2003) and the Museum of Contemporary Art, Chicago (2000).

Mathieu Lehanneur graduated from ENSCI-Les Ateliers in 2001. He is currently exploring possibilities in nature and technology for their breakthrough potential in functions and their capacity to work magic. He made his international debut with a series entitled 'Elements' (for which he was awarded the VIA Carte blanche in 2006) and the 'Bel Air' filtering system for plants (2007), six objects that form a domestic 'Health Angels' kit for rebalancing everyday physiological needs (such as lack of sunlight in winter) and countering aggression factors in urban settings (noise and air pollution).

Sean Lally founded the office WEATHERS to embrace the potential overlap between the disciplines of architecture, landscape architecture and urban design. He was a visiting instructor at UCLA, and an assistant professor at the Rice School of Architecture before recently joining UIC's School of Architecture as an assistant professor in 2009. He is co-editor (with Jessica Young) of *SOFTSPACE: From a Representation of Form to a Simulation of Space* (Routledge, 2007).

An Te Liu is Associate Professor at the John H Daniels Faculty of Architecture, University of Toronto. He has been awarded the Berlin Residency in the Visual Arts by the Canada Council for the Arts. A monograph on his work, *Matter*, has recently been published by the Künstlerhaus Bethanien.

Zbigniew Oksiuta is an artist, architect and scientist who experiments with the possibility of designing biological structures. He studied architecture at Warsaw Polytechnic, and his work has been shown at venues around the world including the Venice Biennale of Architecture (2004), the ArchiLab d'Orleans (2004), Ars Electronica (Linz, 2007), the Biennale of Electronic Arts (Perth, 2007), Center for Contemporary Art (Warsaw, 2007) and the FACT Foundation for Arts and Creative Technology (Liverpool, 2008). He lives and works in Cologne.

Philippe Rahm obtained his architectural degree in 1993 at the EPFL in Switzerland. His office for architecture currently works in Paris and Lausanne on several private and public projects in France, Poland, Italy and Austria. He has exhibited at Archilab (2000), SF-MoMA (2001), the Centre Pompidou (2007), and the Venice Biennale (2008). He was Headmaster at the AA School in London and has lectured at schools including the Cooper Union, Harvard School of Design, UCLA and Princeton.

Mason White is Assistant Professor at the University of Toronto Faculty of Architecture, Landscape and Design where he runs the InfraNet Lab. He is also a founding partner of Lateral Office.

AD+

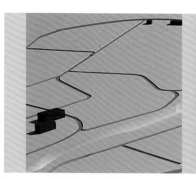 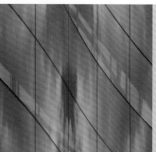   

CONTENTS

Kings Place
Hall One

When is an office development more than office space? Howard Watson describes how through the inclusion of two small auditoria in the basement of Kings Place in London King's Cross, Dixon Jones was able to create a true mixture of amenities while responding to the area's cultural needs and eclipsing its reputation for being less than salubrious.

Dixon Jones has been heavily involved in the redevelopment of London's major cultural repositories, including the Royal Opera House, the National Gallery, the National Portrait Gallery and Somerset House, but Kings Place in King's Cross offered the practice the opportunity to conjure cultural architecture right from its foundations. Housed within a mixed-use development (comprising 26,000 square metres/279,862 square feet of office space, galleries and two auditoria, all designed by Dixon Jones), Hall One is the first purpose-built concert hall in London since 1982.

The extreme rarity of the opportunity, combined with the status of London as one of the most important classical music centres in the world, could have pushed Dixon Jones towards wanton experimentation with the concert-hall form. Furthermore, the purpose of the whole development was ambitious and headline grabbing. According to architect Jeremy Dixon of Dixon Jones, the intention of the Kings Place developer Peter Millican was 'to ask "Why isn't an office building a more public space?" It is an experiment. Can an office building be a proper cultural building, part of city life?' It is fair to say that an affirmative answer to the latter question, and the ambitious intentions of both the developer and the architects, rest on the success of Hall One, the relatively small auditorium right in the base of the project. It is from here that the cultural purpose of the complex must be projected beyond the confines of the city and out to the international performers and audiences that need to be coaxed to King's Cross in order for the project to truly succeed on an artistic level.

King's Cross, the formerly dark, characterful but seedy area of London, more famous for prostitution than cultural endeavour, is

Dixon Jones, Hall One, Kings Place, London, 2008
Hall One of Kings Place is situated in the basement of a new mixed-use office and cultural building in King's Cross, an area of London currently undergoing extensive redevelopment. The section shows the acoustically driven variation of the oak decoration, with spaced pillars in the upper section and irregularly angled recesses just below, followed by narrow horizontal bands and irregular vertical strips towards the base.

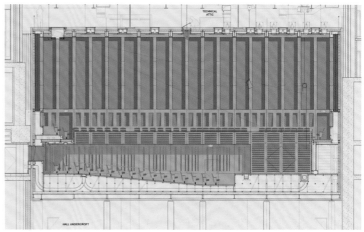

Dixon Jones, Hall One, Kings Place, London, 2008

above: Approach to the entrance of Hall One, from the foyer, showing the gallery level above.

right: The roadside facade, featuring an undulating, triple-layered wave of glass.

opposite: The curving restaurant on the ground floor of the rotunda. The joint restaurant and bar area, which overlooks the canal, makes good use of the architectural form, with a curved Brazilian granite bar counter, smoked oak and granite flooring and, in the bar section, tall, slim, curved, light-oak bar tables which offer some synchronicity with the design of Hall One.

undergoing extensive redevelopment – detractors, including lovers of urban grit and, presumably, former clients, could more harshly describe the overhaul as urban sanitisation. Kings Place, which replaces some warehousing and a public house, forms a triumvirate of new projects with the reborn St Pancras station (now London's terminal for Eurostar trains) and the Regent Quarter, a self-styled 'retail and leisure hub'. Just above the Regent Quarter on York Way, Kings Place is announced by a huge, rippling wave of glazing. By contrast, its side and rear are dressed in mellow, Jura limestone. The glazing and the huge openings at the base of the most notable architectural feature, an eight-storey rotunda which parallels the curve of the canal at its foot, express Millican's desire to make this a public, accessible building. The development has indubitably reinvigorated this formerly foreboding section of the canal and offers waterside strollers easy access to the building's amenities.

Inside, the atrium rises up the full height of the building and makes a monumental feature of the interior curve of the rotunda. While access to the offices (housing the *Guardian* newspaper staff) is through a distinct, wood-panelled reception area, the atrium, gallery and concert foyer for entrance into the two auditoria feature plain white plastered walls and floors

of fossilised Jura limestone which, in contrast to the exterior, has been cut with the grain and highly polished. Broad escalators lead into the spacious well of the building, which is surrounded by exhibition space. Jeremy Dixon worried about synchronising the usually compartmentalised worlds of gallery and concert-going, but the combination allows the journey towards the auditoria to become a welcome theatrical prelude – purists be damned!

The smaller auditorium, Hall Two, is a wood-panelled, flexible performance and rehearsal space, not without its own architectural merits, but the true joy of the entire complex is Hall One. Dixon Jones may have leapt at the opportunity to design a concert hall from scratch, but the design is a true amalgam between aesthetic desire and acoustic need. It may be a surprise that a practice given free rein has returned to investigate the traditional shoebox shape of the concert-hall type, but this is the result of extensive acoustic research rather than a wish to pursue design orthodoxy. The detail, too, is born out of a wish to marry design innovation with acoustic perfection. Dixon says: 'Architects tend to prefer regularity, but acoustic distribution is better by random design. The solution was to create a subtle variety within the decoration that would suit the acoustic.' Consequently, Paul Jolly, Dixon Jones' project architect for Hall One, and Rob Harris from Arup Acoustics needed to work hand-in-glove; fortunately for both the eyes and sensitive ears of the concert-goer, the union of disciplines was harmonious.

The 610-tonne (600-ton), 420-seat double cube, which floats on rubber pads to virtually obliterate noise transfer, is a serene oak box

Dixon Jones, Hall One, Kings Place, London, 2008
Axonometric view of the underground hall, situated in a 25-metre (82-foot) deep propped basement beneath the main building.

that manages an interesting interplay between larger-scale order and more intricate and random decoration towards its base. The grid of the steel structure is most obvious in the upper part, where the oak-veneered columns and a coffered ceiling provide an orderly regimentation. The columns, which break up longer sound waves, are set slightly away from the grey, smooth-plastered walls. This gap is functional, allowing continuous curtains to be drawn around the walls for spoken performances where the acoustics need to be softened, but also provides an unusual aesthetic, giving the sense that the soft-blue lit grey plaster is an infinite sky beyond a free-standing cage – a notable achievement in an underground space. Below the columns there is a strip of irregularly angled, rectangular recesses, which augment the even distribution of high frequencies, and a continuous balcony, which introduces a necessary intimacy to the concert hall.

The raked main seating area and the stage are almost completely encased in oak, with an apparently regular, horizontal, inset pattern around the stage giving way to the random spacing and depths of vertical incisions around the stalls. The dark-grey padded seats, which continue the light oak-theme through their curving wooden backs, were carefully acoustically tested before the positioning and rake were determined. All the oak veneer required, including that for Hall Two, has been cut from a single 500-year-old tree.

Dixon says: 'For me, attending a performance must be about the whole thing. You are skating on thin ice if you do anything to break the mood of the performance' – the integration of the highest possible acoustic sensibility within an ordered, serene design ensures that there is no screech or rumble, either visual or aural, to disrupt the harmony. Depending on the right scheduling, there is likely to be a well-trodden path from St Pancras to Hall One. Δ+

Canalside view of the rotunda, across the water from a warehouse building more typical of the King's Cross area.

Interior of Hall One; view from the stage. The entire oak veneer of the interior, covering the walls, balcony fronts, pillars and seat backs, is cut from a single oak. The whole development aims to be environmentally sustainable.

Howard Watson is an author, journalist and editor based in London. He is co-author, with Eleanor Curtis, of the new 2nd edition of *Fashion Retail* (Wiley-Academy, 2007), £34.99. See www.wiley.com. Previous books include *The Design Mix: Bars, Cocktails and Style* (2006) and *Hotel Revolution: 21st-Century Hotel Design* (2005), both also published by Wiley-Academy.

Mark Yoes, Claire Weisz and Layng Pew at the Weisz + Yoes (WXY architecture + urban design) offices on Centre Street in Chinatown, Manhattan.

Weisz + Yoes (WXY architecture + urban design)

Few small avant-garde practices have an impact on visitors to New York like that of WXY, as the firm is sometimes called. Theirs is particularly surprising since, as **Jayne Merkel** notes, they have only completed a handful of freestanding buildings. But this mid-career husband-and-wife team of Claire Weisz and Mark Yoes – and their new partner, Layng Pew, whom they met at Yale 20 years ago – are changing the face of Times Square and redesigning historic Battery Park at the southern tip of Manhattan where ferries leave for the Statue of Liberty and Ellis Island. These heavily used public places are only the most recent ones that they have inventively improved over the last decade and a half.

Claire Weisz's forays into community design began when the first of her three daughters was born 16 years ago. She left her job at Agrest and Gandelsonas and formed a partnership with Ursula Warchol, a young architect who also had a child and lived in the loft next to hers. It was the depths of the 1990s recession, and their neighbourhood park at Thompson and Spring Streets in SoHo was a shambles. So they put together a co-op with other young families who lived nearby, fixed up the park house (which was used by the lifeguards in summer), and created an open school there. They also planted the grounds, and painted a mural by the pool.

Some of Weisz and Warchol's first clients came from that ad hoc group of artists, designers and photographers. Their most spectacular project was a boutique in SoHo for the dress designer J Morgan Puett, which looked like the backstage of a theatre. Eventually Warchol gave up architecture to produce handmade books and moved to eastern Pennsylvania with her husband, architectural photographer Paul Warchol, and their children. Weisz's husband Mark Yoes, who had been moonlighting with Weisz and Warchol after his day job at the Pei Partnership, left that office in 1998, and they founded Weisz + Yoes, supporting the practice partly with Weisz's teaching at Pratt Institute, the City University of New York, New Jersey Institute of Technology and Columbia.

A small, temporary visitors centre for the hexagonal granite Museum of Jewish Heritage designed by Kevin Roche, in Battery Park City, was the first building that brought the young firm acclaim. Paul Goldberger called it 'The Little Pavilion That Could' in *The New Yorker*. 'The building in question is one of Battery Park City's most admired, if tiniest, gems,' he wrote. 'The little glass pavilion wasn't in most guidebooks, but in time it became the part of the museum complex that architects, especially younger ones talked about. In a city with few strong modern public buildings, it was a kind of minor underground icon.'[1]

Although it only stood for a few years (until Roche could add an entry pavilion of his own), the visitors centre proved that these architects could make a major impact with a small structure – or no structure at all. And since that time, a significant part of their practice (besides the usual houses and apartments) has involved public space. For four years at the end of the 1990s, before becoming a professor of urban design at New York University, Weisz was a co-director of the nonprofit Design Trust for Public Space with Andrea Woodner, the founder. The two had met a few years before when Weisz received a fellowship from Woodner's Center for Public Architecture to study opportunities for 'Sports and the City' on Randalls and Wards Islands, just northeast of Manhattan, which over the years had housed hospitals, indigents, orphans and recreational facilities. Weisz's work with Woodner at the Design Trust furthered her interest in community design – and had a very significant influence on the city. Together they paved the way for the 'greening' of New York by creating the High Performance Building Guidelines for the city's Department of Design and Construction, instigating the High Line park now being designed

Weisz + Yoes, Temporary visitors centre, Museum of Jewish Heritage, Battery Park City, New York, 2002
left: This elegant, light-filled entry pavilion managed to hold its own in the landscape without upstaging the massive granite hexagon of a museum it was built to accommodate until that building's own space for staff offices, ticketing, package check and security screening could be built. The modest yet handsome little structure, built in four months on a minimal budget, was composed of a pair of offset trapezoids, one sheathed in glass, the other in lead-coated copper roofing.

Weisz + Yoes, NYC Information Center, Manhattan, 2009
opposite: This cool white high-tech visitors centre has built-in electronic maps and kiosks for visitors to plan their days in New York. These personalised intineraries can be printed out or sent to their mobile phones. Electronic images portray the city on a big TV screen, but there are also brochures of numerous kinds tucked into handy pocket mouldings running along the walls.

Weisz + Yoes with Buro Happold Engineers, Bronx Charter School for the Arts, The Bronx, New York, 2006
This conversion of a pair of warehouses maintained the colourful exterior typical of the postindustrial neighbourhood, but provided some of the dignity appropriate to a school by sheathing it in an irregular abstract pattern of coloured tiles and creating a facade with a stepped entrance where the loading dock once stood.

The loft-like feel of this lively school was created by using industrial materials and bright colours, and introducing natural light through north-facing clerestories. Most classrooms have glass interior walls so the light enters public spaces and gives the school an open feel. Since there was no money for lockers, hooks and cubbyholes hold students' stuff.

Weisz + Yoes with West 8, New York Aquarium Perimeter Design Competition, Coney Island, Brooklyn, New York, 2007
Intended to encourage casual visitors to the Coney Island boardwalk to go to the aquarium and those visiting the aquarium to experience the ocean nearby, this project has an engineered 'living' dune landscape, which also gives the aquarium a dramatic and iconic perimeter that doubles as an interactive exhibit. There is also a coral-inspired retaining wall, and an 18.2-metre (60-foot) high jellyfish pavilion which would give this institution a presence that embraces the uniqueness of its site on the water at Coney Island.

by Diller Scofidio + Renfro with Field Operations, and conducting an extensive study of threatened community gardens to encourage their preservation. In the process they worked with neighbourhood groups throughout New York's five boroughs. Wander around parks and public spaces with Weisz and you will meet everyone from grateful maintenance workers to school principals to people who live nearby. But what you see there will be the product of a very sensitive visual intelligence that Weisz and Yoes share. He is the one with a particular sensitivity to colour. She finds new talents in the design community – before they are famous. Weisz and Yoes both believe in taking formal and visual risks. And new partner Layng Pew makes sure the risks are not in technical areas or construction techniques that will cause problems down the line. He also knows how to negotiate with all the agencies that have to be on board to accomplish anything in New York.

In 1999, Weisz + Yoes was one of a dozen avant-garde young or mid-career practices selected by the New York City Housing Authority to design innovative community centres at traditional tower-in-the-park public housing complexes. Among the five they worked on was the Van Dyke Community Center in Brownsville, Brooklyn, with Olhausen DuBois Architects and Ken Smith landscape architect. This helped fill up difficult-to-secure open space between the towers with a generous curved, glass-walled addition that serves as both a corridor and informal meeting place. Its arc-shaped roof echoes the curve of the plan and the ceiling vault behind it, updating the complex, adding a bit of glamour and providing a safe place for residents to congregate.[2]

Weisz's involvement with members of the Bronx community led to the firm's commission to design the acclaimed Bronx Charter School for the Arts. Their work encompassed a good deal more than the conversion of single-storey warehouses to an unusually innovative arts-oriented school for children from ages four to ten. The architects were involved in the community, conceptual and physical planning of the colourful below-low-budget school (the cheapest in all of New York) where students from throughout the Bronx are selected by lottery as so many want to enrol. (Now, plans for middle and upper schools are in the works.) Two adjacent buildings were combined. An old raised loading dock was converted to a stepped central entrance. The buildings were sheathed in tiles arranged in vertical stripes of various sizes in bright colours like those painted on the nearby car repair shops, food distribution centres and storage facilities. The abstract pattern, repeated on linoleum floors inside, helps orient students to different areas. The old roof was replaced with a series of north-facing clerestories that bring natural light into the building which has only a few windows – except on interior classroom walls facing corridors and the big open central space where administrators work in a low-walled cubicle within easy view of arriving students. The colourful palette of the floors and outside walls is echoed in the school uniforms, which consist of T-shirts in a wide variety of colours imprinted with 'Bronx Charter School for the Arts'. Students can wear any colour T-shirt on any day, so there is always an ever-changing pattern in all the halls and classrooms.

The purposeful playfulness of this school permeates the parks and urban design projects WXY are involved with today. 'I think when you do work that is public,

there is no real distinction between architecture and urban design,' Weisz notes, adding that what makes it different is that budget constraints are greater and construction takes longer. But the rewards are incalculable.

Today the architects are working on waterfront parks in Greenpoint and Williamsburg, Brooklyn; a brownfield remediation site in the Bronx; a garage and salt shed for the Department of Sanitation in Manhattan; an ambulance station in the Bronx; a school for autistic children in New Jersey; and a dramatic new plaza for Cooper Square and Astor Place where Eighth and Lafayette streets, Broadway and Fourth Avenue converge.

The most dramatic effect Weisz + Yoes will have on the city, though, is in the Times Square area where they recently completed the new high-tech NYC Information Center, are repaving the heavily travelled streets and pedestrian islands in Times Square itself, and will be working on the Times Square Information Center in the historic Embassy Theater on Seventh Avenue and 47th Street for the Times Square Alliance. Unlike the NYC Information Center, which provides information about all kinds of activities in the entire New York area,

Weisz + Yoes with Mathews Nielsen Landscape Architecture, Monsignor John J Kowsky Plaza, Battery Park City, New York, 2005
Located over the pump house for the World Trade Center, which will now be used for the memorials, parts of the ground must be opened and serviced occasionally, but this project has reclaimed the land for community space with a shaded plaza overlooking the nearby Hudson River, a sandbox play area for young children and a popular dog run.

Weisz + Yoes with EDAW Inc, Zipper Bench prototype for the Greenpoint-Williamsburg Waterfront Park Masterplan, Brooklyn, New York, 2009
The design standards for this 3.2-kilometre (2-mile) long esplanade and conceptual framework for 11 hectares (28 acres) of waterfront park in two redeveloping neighbourhoods facing the East River and Manhattan is part of a citywide plan for riverfront development. The reflective stainless-steel benches and railings, which relate to the curved water's edge and the movement of water, will also be used at other parks around the city.

Weisz + Yoes with Piet Oudolf and Starr Whitehouse Landscape Architects and Planners, Battery Park Bosque, The Battery, Lower Manhattan, New York, 2005
Battery Park occupies the southern tip of Manhattan where the first Dutch settlement was founded. A circular stone fort, built between 1808 and 1811 to guard against British invasion, later housed a restaurant, theatre and aquarium, and now serves as a museum and ticket office for the Statue of Liberty and Ellis Island. The surrounding park, which echoes the forms of the fort with a series of spirals, has been naturalistically reinvigorated by the architects who have opened up views of the harbour, added plantings similar to the original marshes and forests, and created a walk-in fountain and a series of curvaceous benches and kiosks.

Weisz + Yoes, Times Square Redesign, New York, 2009
This renovation of the pedestrian spaces in Times Square will increase the width of the sidewalks and expand the public space in Duffy Square where a new red glass-walled TKTS booth offers half-price theatre tickets and stepped seating theatre. The new abstract pavement pattern on black granite will both absorb the lights of Times Square in some areas and reflect them in others, creating a syncopated pattern in the spirit of the exciting but sometimes disorienting theatre district to unify the chaotic area invitingly.

Weisz + Yoes with Dattner Architects, Department of Sanitation garage and salt shed, Manhattan, New York, 2009
This building for the storage and repair of garbage trucks as well as Department of Sanitation offices has a louvred facade differentiated on each elevation to designate the different functions and relate to the surrounding neighbourhood. Exciting architecture is essential in this former industrial area which is becoming increasingly residential, as people who live nearby want the services of the sanitation department but don't want its facilities in their own backyards.

the Times Square centre will provide a place for tourists to relax and learn about theatrical events in the Times Square area itself.

The project that will probably make the greatest impact is the partially completed redesign of historic Battery Park, where New York City was first settled. The architects have reinforced the park's original but long-obscured spiral pattern that relates to Castle Clinton, the historic fort that serves as a ticketing area for boat trips to the Statue of Liberty and the Ellis Island Immigration Museum. They have opened up waterfront views of the harbour, created low curving benches to fit into the raw naturalistic landscape design for the verdant Battery Bosque area of the park planted by Dutch garden designer Piet Oudolf, and designed a spiralling carousel which will have glowing, glass sea creatures instead of wooden horses for children to ride on when it opens next year. There is also a new circular fountain that visitors can walk through, play spaces and kiosks for snacks – all integrated within the seaside atmosphere of the bosque itself.

What is interesting is that none of these architects who are changing the most visible faces of New York are natives. Weisz grew up in Edmonton, Alberta (in western Canada), Yoes in Houston, Texas, and Pew in

Philadelphia. The famous *New Yorker* magazine writer EB White famously once wrote: 'There are roughly three New Yorks. There is, first, the New York of the man or woman who was born there, who takes the city for granted and accepts its size, its turbulence as natural and inevitable. Second, there is the New York of the commuter – the city that is devoured by locusts each day and spat out each night. Third, there is the New York of the person who was born somewhere else and came to New York in quest of something. Of these trembling cities the greatest is the last – the city of final destination, the city that is a goal. It is this third city that accounts for New York's high strung disposition, its poetical deportment, its dedication to the arts, and its incomparable achievements.'[3] This is the New York that these three 'immigrants' are both taming and invigorating. ⊅+

Notes
1. Paul Goldberger, 'The Little Pavilion that Could', *The New Yorker*, 21 January 2002, p 26.
2. See Jayne Merkel, 'Fine Tuning: How the New York City Housing Authority Makes Housing Work', *Architectural Design, Home Front: New Developments in Housing*, July/August 2003, pp 70–81.
3. EB White, *Here Is New York*, Harper and Brothers (New York), 1949, p 1 (from the opening passage).

The Royal Institution

Farrells, The Royal Institution of Great Britain, London, 2008
The new glazed addition at the rear of the Royal Institution creates a zone that offers both horizontal and vertical circulation.

David Littlefield describes how Sir Terry Farrell's rethinking of the Royal Institution in Mayfair has led to a rationalisation and redesign that has transformed the premises from a tatty Georgian labyrinth into an airy series of modern spaces, Farrell having effectively re-imagined 'the building while retaining the essence of what made it special in the first place'.

A piece of trivia: London's first one-way traffic system is located on Albermarle Street, just off Piccadilly. The reason? Scientific lectures at the Royal Institution of Great Britain proved so popular that horse-drawn traffic was thrown into chaos. Today the RI is one of London's most venerable, and perhaps least known, institutions; but a £22 million tidying up exercise by Sir Terry Farrell might well lodge this august building back in the public consciousness. Which is exactly where it deserves to be.

The RI was founded in 1799 as a place for 'diffusing the knowledge and facilitating the general introduction of useful mechanical inventions and improvements, and for teaching by courses of philosophical lectures and experiments the application of science to the common purposes of life'. For two centuries the institution has done rather better than that, and scientists working in its laboratories have discovered no less than 10 chemical elements. Fourteen people with a strong RI link have been awarded Nobel prizes. If you want to see the equipment Michael Faraday used for his electromagnetic experiments, or the glassware John Tyndall employed to work out why the sky is blue, it is to be found on Albermarle Street. So too are early examples of the Davy lamp, invented by Humphrey Davy to allow miners to work underground by the light of a naked flame without the risk of causing an explosion; laser gear that helped fathom how CFCs break

down the ozone layer is also numbered among the RI's list of extraordinary scientific artefacts. The Royal Institution is quite a place.

The RI was installed in a row of houses designed, at least in part, by John Carr – an architect who practised mainly in the north of England, particularly in York where he was twice lord mayor. In 1838 the terrace was given a monumental facade by Lewis Vulliamy, modelled on the Temple of Antoninus in Rome. Behind this pompous facade of Corinthian columns, however, lay a series of rooms that had, over the years, become uninviting, poorly connected, tired and tatty. In the best traditions of scientific endeavour, the building was an unkempt labyrinth of clutter, and despite the fact that the RI has always been a public building it did not appear that way. To the average passer-by, it signalled privacy and aloofness. Farrell says the building reminded him of a grand country house that had been occupied by the army during the war and abandoned ever since. His interventions have changed all that.

There is now a logic to the place; circulation has been reinvented; the difference between public and private spaces is clearly demarcated; there is now a brightness, a freshness and a certain modernity running through the building. There are also places for coffee. The really clever element of this work, though, has been to thoroughly reimagine the building while retaining the essence of what made it special in the first place; it still retains the air of a row of terrace houses that have been knocked through, and the decor changes abruptly from one space to the next. Edwardian opulence here, illuminated graphics there; grand Georgian staircase out front; glass lift out back. Every single room and antechamber has a character all its

The grand facade of the Royal Institution has always suggested an interior of large, expansive rooms and grand corridors. That was far from the truth, however.

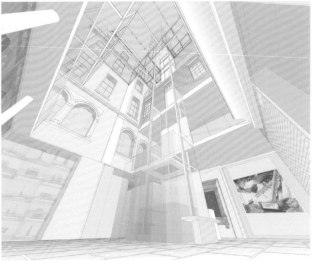

Farrell's big architectural gesture was to rehabilitate a rear courtyard of shabby sheds and workshops, glazing it over and bringing it inside.

own, and walking through the RI still feels like an exploration even though its zoning is eminently straightforward and sensible.

Typically, Farrell and his team began by drawing diagrams of the building. The aim was to create clear horizontal and vertical connections and sort out the jumble of functions that included a lecture theatre, libraries, laboratories, offices and exhibition spaces. There was even what staff called the 'sad stair' at the southern end of the building, so called because of its neglect. 'Organisationally, it had a lot of problems,' says Farrell. He talks about 'mental maps', imaginary models of buildings or places in which it is simple to locate oneself. The mental map of the RI now looks something like this: a ground floor of interconnected public spaces for socialising, eating, meeting and drinking; a subground

'What we've got now is a building which looks and feels like its got twice as much space and volume,' says Farrell.

public exhibition space; a first-floor lecture theatre and library suite; and third-floor offices, above which sit laboratories. The key to such straightforward zoning was provided by rehabilitating a rear courtyard of shabby sheds and workshops, glazing it over and bringing it inside. 'What we've got now is a building which looks and feels like its got twice as much space and volume,' says Farrell.

Some of the spaces Farrell has rescued are simply delightful, including the Cartier jewellery shop and its timber-panelled workshop that have become the Time and Space bar. The original grand staircase has been spruced up and its ceiling relieved of accretions of cream paint and restored to Georgian blue. Better than that is the way a stone memorial plaque that sat at the turn of the stair has been replaced by a little arched window which looks through to the gathering space beyond, with its multicoloured '10/14' wall celebrating those chemical elements and the Nobel prizes. The change had to be agreed with English Heritage, but it is a move which (all on its own) speaks eloquently of the shift that has taken place within this building – a little less veneration and a little more zest. Even the first-floor carpet neatly incorporates the pattern created by iron filings around the poles of a magnet.

PREVIOUS USE ARRANGEMENT

	CARETAKER			L4
	OFFICE + LABS			L3
FARADAY THEATRE	DIRECTOR		OFFICE	L2
	LIBRARY + MEETING			L1
LECTURE	ENTRANCE	MEETING	OTHER	STREET
LAB	ARCHIVE + EXHIBITION		OTHER	GF

NEW USE ARRANGEMENT 'THE SCHEME'

	DIRECTOR			L4
	OFFICE + LAB			L3
FARADAY THEATRE	RI OFFICE			L2
	LIBRARY, MEETING + HERITAGE			L1
WC's	ENTRANCE + HOSPITALITY			STREET
YSC	ARCHIVE + EXHIBITION		KITCHEN	GF

Terry Farrell zoning diagrams showing the organisation of the RI building before and after the £22 million remodelling. The new schematic for the building is much more horizontal, locating specific functions on their own floors.

The main gathering space behind the main entrance. This '10/14' wall celebrates the 10 chemical elements and 14 Nobel prizes with which the RI is associated.

The main entrance, illustrating the
new internal window at the turn
of the stair, through which the
'10/14' wall can be glimpsed.

The remodelled lecture theatre equipped with large, more generous seats (to a new colour scheme). RI lectures have always been dynamic affairs, with practical demonstrations of theory.

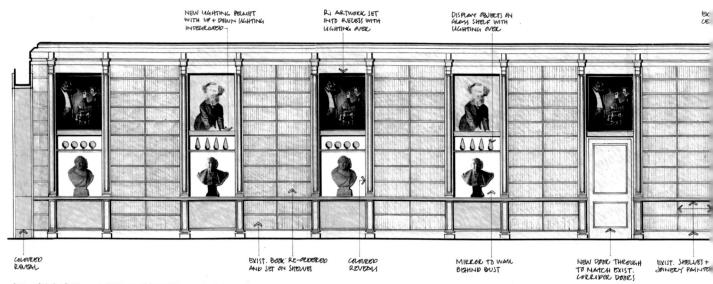

RED CORRIDOR · WEST ELEVATION · SC 1:25 @ A3 HEIGHT

Scientific reference is liberally showered throughout the building, and it is here that the intelligence of the project is in danger of breaking down. Science is, of course, a subject so broad and fascinating that extracting allusions, references and analogies is relatively simple. The form of the rather wonderful chandelier which now hangs over the rehabilitated 'sad stair' is based on the crystalline structure of salt, for example. That, and the magnetic-field reference in the carpet pattern, stay on the right side of subtlety. Other features seem more heavy-handed. The new café at the rear of the building contains a metal spiral, suspended from the ceiling, on which all sorts of scientific paraphernalia are hung. This is rather unnecessary; so, too, are similar displays of lenses and laboratory bits and bobs which hang in glass boxes set over key doorways. The basement now contains an effective exhibition of unlikely artefacts and their stories – Michael Faraday tried (unsuccessfully) to learn the art of making flawless glass and his experimental pieces are on display. Hanging scientific instruments from the ceiling, unlabelled, borders on irreverence – or at least whimsy. The argument, one imagines, is that setting these objects in the light of day is preferable to boxing them up, unseen, in archives. Maybe, but Farrell's biggest contribution to the success of this building is in his deft handling of space rather than the decor. And for that, the scientific establishment and the visiting public are in his debt. ⌂+

David Littlefield is an architectural writer. He has written and edited a number of books, including *Architectural Voices: Listening to Old Buildings*, published by John Wiley & Sons (October 2007). He was also the curator of the exhibition 'Unseen Hands: 100 Years of Structural Engineering', which ran at the Victoria & Albert Museum in 2008. He has taught at Chelsea College of Art & Design and the University of Bath, and is currently a visiting tutor at the University of the West of England.

The 'sad stair' at one end of the building, so called because it had always been forlorn and neglected, has been reinvigorated with the addition of a chandelier modelled on the crystalline structure of salt.

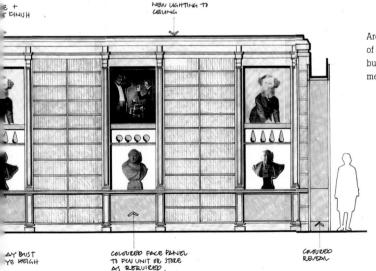

Architects' drawing of the 'red corridor', one of the principal horizontal routes through the building, linking the theatre with library, meeting and heritage spaces.

Articulating Environmental Grounds

A new generation of thinking is emerging in the manipulation of ground systems that, with the aid of parametrics, is enabling a new level of design precision and ecological calibration. **Anne Save de Beaurecueil and Franklin Lee** describe how with Diploma Unit 2 at the Architectural Association in London, they are working towards their goal of fusing architecture, landscape and contemporary art through an engagement with articulated ground organisations.

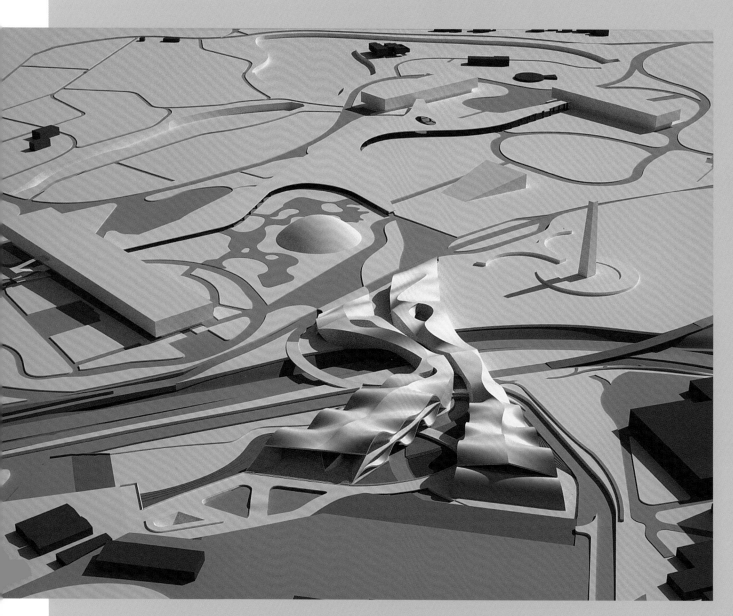

Suyeon Song (AA Diploma Unit 2), Shell Diffusions, Ibirapuera Park, São Paulo, Brazil, 2008
A multiple-scaled corrugated ground system diffuses light, ventilation and pedestrian flows as it connects across the highway separating the two sides of the park.

Maya Carni (AA Diploma Unit 2), Amazon River Micro-Exchange and Demonstration Centre, Belém do Pará, Brazil, 2007
Along the Amazon River's edge, tapered channels promote increased wind ventilation and are calibrated with light-reflector diffusers to cool and illuminate market halls and meeting rooms within.

Yoon Han (AA Diploma Unit 2), Climatic Curves, Ibirapuera Park, São Paulo, Brazil, 2008
A proliferation of folded-baffle components are defined by different plays of tension and compression, creating different degrees of aperture, baffle depth and their corresponding environmental effects, as well as varying degrees of overall arching curvature that structure the bridge formation.

The research conducted by Diploma Unit 2 at the Architectural Association (AA) School of Architecture has focused on the mediation of both environmental and cultural flows, which involved defining a new aesthetic and social agenda for conventional ecological design strategies. The unit has worked not only on designing environmental mitigation systems, but on also synchronising these with programme-circulation organisations, or 'ground' systems, to alleviate the climatic, circulatory and social stagnation that afflicts many global cities. The goal has been to create a fusion between architecture, infrastructure, landscape and contemporary art by articulating ground systems to mediate climatic forces, in the creation of an 'environmental flow choreography'.

Influenced by the philosophical framework established by designers such as Oscar Niemeyer, the 'topological architecture' that emerged in the 1990s explored the manipulation of ground organisations to enable smooth flows and connections between diverse programmes and cultures. Yet to a certain extent, the physical realisation of these ground projects lacked a smaller-scale, more refined resolution for other types of building performances, such as the mediation of climatic forces. With technological development, scripted parametric systems today have brought about a sophisticated level of smaller-scale precision and control to calibrate these environmental forces. However, somehow in this technological advancement, which is often characterised by a ubiquitous proliferation of components for performative roof and wall systems, the systematisation of ground has, in many cases, been largely underemphasised.

Thus, the premise of the research has been to find ways to mediate between both technological performance and the manipulation of grounds for social organisation. Technically, the unit has worked to merge cultural and environmental effects by negotiating between both monolithic surfaces and the articulated strategies of current component-based design. Monolithic surfaces have proven to be more effective for channelling wind and circulation, while component propagation is highly instrumental in sunlight mediation and processes of fabrication. The aim was to create multiscalar transformations of monolithic organisations, introducing variable-component logics, while maintaining some of the fluidity of continuous-surface design strategies.

Articulating Edges

Articulated ground organisations have been used to create new connectivity at impermeable edge conditions. The Shell Diffusions project by Suyeon Song created a cultural complex employing an inhabitable ground-bridge network to reactivate the isolated cultural campus of the existing Oscar Niemeyer Ibirapuera Park in São Paulo, Brazil. The project made micromediations of macro organisations by transforming the raised shell-structure type. This methodology negotiated between 'smooth' surfaces, to create new accessibility for pedestrians, as well as iterative component strategies, to create a new accessibility for diffused light and natural ventilation. Also bridging between the existing buildings of the Ibirapuera Park, the Climatic Curves project by Yoon Han created a dialogue between componentry and circulation with a multiple-bridge network structure that modulated sunlight and ventilation and housed supplementary museum programmes. Addressing the more extreme environmental and social problems at the gateway of the Amazon Forest, Maya Carni's Micro-Exchange and Demonstration Centre along the Amazon River's edge in Belém do Pará, Brazil, created a complex to facilitate an alternative economy between indigenous producers of sustainable rainforest products and foreign investors, so as to counter deforestation. Calibrated with differentiated membrane light reflectors, tapering channels induced natural wind ventilation, as well as the movement of pedestrian and economic flows.

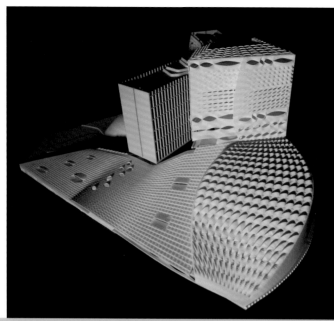

Arthur Mamou-Mani (AA Diploma Unit 2), Light-Ground Transformations of the Headquarters Communist Party, Paris, France, 2008
Curving, delaminating ground and component systems create a new accessibility for public programmes and calibrated lighting effects.

Asako Hayashi (AA Diploma Unit 2), Double Ground-Double Skin Museum Interface, Ibirapuera Park, São Paulo, Brazil, 2008
The existing Niemeyer Department of Transportation Hall is transformed with a new climatic buffer zone that mediates reflected light and gallery sequences.

Articulating Monoliths

New cultural and environmental accessibility was created in the articulation of monolithic ground constructs. Arthur Mamou-Mani's Light-Ground Transformations of the Headquarters of the Communist Party project in Paris achieved this through the introduction of a building extension to hold new public programmes, mediated by a new environmental component system. To counter the tyrannical image of the party's headquarters, the new complex would embody a fluid, decentralised design open to mediated flows of capital and climate by rigorously calibrating and diffusing their effects. In a similar fashion, Ying Wang's Porosity Generator for a Walled City project in Xian, China, uses circulatory and climatic mediators to dissipate the city's fortress walls. Tectonically, this new museum project redefined the monolithic wall and threshold gateway types by transforming them into a meandering ramping system, bringing a new porosity for pedestrian and environmental flows. Finally, Asako Hayashi's Double Ground-Double Skin Museum Interface project brings new circulatory and ecological performances to Oscar Niemeyer's Department of Transportation Hall in the Ibirapuera Park. A double skin was scripted to respond parametrically to the influences of the sun, and to support a new path system that was interconnected with a double-ground pedestrian bridge.

Ying Wang (AA Diploma Unit 2), Porosity Generator for a Walled City, Xian, China, 2008
Multiple-ramp systems produce a new circulatory and environmental porosity for the fortress wall condition.

Emmanouil Matsis (AA Diploma Unit 2), Articulated Residual System, Ibirapuera Park, São Paulo, Brazil, 2008
Sculpted ground and bridging connections diffuse sound and light for a system of open market-gallery paths between the residual spaces of the park.

Charlotte Thomas (AA Diploma Unit 2), Vascular Attraction Mediators, Ibirapuera Park, São Paulo, Brazil, 2008
Attraction scripts synchronise wind, light and circulation flows in bundled vertical shafts for a series of interconnected gallery follies.

Articulation Fields

Macroscaled field conditions have been reactivated by new micro-ground systems. The Vascular Attraction Mediators project by Charlotte Thomas employed multiple-scale attraction field scripting to synchronise the ornamental movement of both cultural and environmental flows for a series of gallery follies in the Ibirapuera Park. In critique of the large-scale, monolithic Expo halls, smaller-scale bundles of vertical channels were aligned to the attraction agents of prevailing sun, wind and circulation flows. These channels served as ventilation air shafts, light-diffusion chimneys and spiralling ramped galleries to create a dialogue between art and the external environment. Also distributed across the park, the Articulated Residual System project by Emmanouil Matsis reorganised the isolated residual spaces between the buildings into a flexible open-market framework. This was achieved by sculpting bermed and bridging ground connections, which were further calibrated with component structures, creating microclimates of mediated sound, lighting and ventilation.

For different programmes and sites, the investigations of the AA Diploma Unit 2 have used an environmental articulation of ground to transform a range of urban contexts. The projects have been informed by a Brazilian cultural context that is characterised by a strong connection with nature, due perhaps to the influence of the country's sculptural, variegated landscapes and its African and Indigenous-Indian traditions on Brazilian society. This has certainly influenced an architectural precedence for the environmental manipulation of different social-ground organisations. Overall, the projects have attempted to create a more symbiotic relationship between urban culture, environmental conditioning and the natural landscape, to bring sustainable architectural methodologies a new civic and cultural relevance. 𝚫+

Anne Save de Beaurecueil and Franklin Lee are Diploma 2 unit masters at the Architectural Association (AA) School of Architecture and co-directors of the SUBdV architecture practice in São Paulo (www.subdv.com). Both have lectured and been published internationally, and their work has been shown at many international exhibitions, most recently at 'Raw, New Brazilian Architecture' at the London Festival of Architecture 2008, and the Beijing Architectural Biennale 2008.

'Unit Factor' is edited by Michael Weinstock, who is Academic Head and Master of Technical Studies at the Architectural Association School of Architecture in London. He is co-guest-editor with Michael Hensel and Achim Menges of the *Emergence: Morphogenetic Design Strategies* (May 2004) and *Techniques and Technologies in Morphogenetic Design* (March 2006) issues of *Architectural Design*. He is currently writing a book on the architecture of emergence for John Wiley & Sons Ltd.

Architecture of Disbelief
Is Architectural Speciation a Good Thing?

Can visionary architects have their cake and eat it, luxuriating in pecuniary success while also continuing to assert their avant-gardism? Neil Spiller attended a conference in Cornell that brought the role of the architectural visionary under the spotlight and gave him much food for thought.

I was lucky enough recently to be invited to be the keynote speaker for a conference at Cornell University. The event was called 'The Architecture of Disbelief' and was ably curated and convened by Mark Morris and Jim Williamson.

Participants included Lebbeus Woods, up-and-coming MIT researcher and designer Neri Oxman, archetypal New Yorker Evan Douglis, British artists with architectural preoccupations Langlands and Bell, Dagmar Richter, cyber-monk Karl Chu and the *agent provocateur* and rascal, Jeff Kipnis.

The three-day event revolved around the questions provoked by visionary architecture. Do we believe in it or not? Notions discussed included: 'Is visionary architecture even possible in the 21st century?', and 'Why is much alleged avant-garde architecture so similar?' Indeed, the older generation of so-called 'visionary architects' have long since gone over to commercial

hackery, yet these same architects still manage to have their cake and eat it. They continue to assert their avant-gardism and simultaneously luxuriate in pecuniary success. An example of Debordian Spectacle, a French Leftist idea developed in the 1950s and 1960s that capitalism assimilates and disables critical opposition by acceptance and recasting to its own goal of social fragmentation. This seems very true in an architectural context.

Jeff Kipnis fulfilled the role of iconoclast and polemicist and framed three questions for us to consider in a round-table discussion that gave the proceedings their finale. These were:

1 Get over it. Can we take the work of the late 1970s/early 1980s as visionary and assign work that is just emerging the same status?

2 Speciation. Why is architecture still interested in the disbelief/belief dichotomy when other disciplines have left those fundamental questions behind in favour of specialisation/speciation (production

of difference versus values)? Does diversity/range of expertise trump critical notions of belief in architecture as a whole? Does speculation work beyond any dialectic?

3 Audience versus constituency. Speculation opens up this question; without a client per se, where does speculative work address itself?

It is Kipnis' issue of speciation that I would like to address here. It can be argued that ubiquitous software, hardware and wetware has created a situation for architects akin to the biological Burgess Shale event. The Shale is a fossil record of a fecund blossoming of thousands of varieties of flora and fauna that took place 500 million years ago. The argument goes that hundreds of different approaches to architecture, structure and form-making, and ecology are now made possible and this will result in new niches in the architectural market. In the fitness landscape comprised of practice and academia, some forms of architecture would survive and mutate; others would become extinct.

However, what I see is a convergence of architectural form-making, spatial aspirations and ambivalence to established global consumerist sociopolitical dynamics. In short, an apathetic convivial compliance to existing modes of operation. Technology merely ubiquitising architectural thought and form. This is a bad thing.

My view has not changed since the early 1990s when I wrote in my book *Digital Dreams* that 'the complacency of some within the architectural profession is very dangerous, for the evolving spatial lexicon is uniquely tailored for an expansion to the architect's role'.[1]

It is not speciation I was arguing for here, but expansion of roles and a creatively challenging remit. Exactly what is in danger of not happening now.

Everything is not culturally equivalent in architecture. Speculative work should address itself to negating the perception of architects as foppish formalists. It should posit new spatial relations. Perhaps the current economic downturn will trigger more inquisitive spatial investigations by architects as such lacunas of economic activities have in the past. Δ+

Neil Spiller is Professor of Architecture and Digital Theory and Vice Dean at the Bartlett, University College London. His article 'Spatial notation and the magical operations of collage in the post-digital age' is to be published in Mark Garcia (ed), *Diagrams of Architecture*, John Wiley & Sons Ltd, May 2009.

Note
1. Neil Spiller, *Digital Dreams: Architecture and the New Alchemic Technologies*, Ellipsis (London) and Watson and Guptill (New York), 1998, p 10.

Lebbeus Woods, Formation 5, undated
I have been a fan of Lebbeus Woods for more than 20 years. I am touched by his humanism and his desire to make his architecture thoughtful and not legislated by outmoded conceptions of what might constitute architecture. This image and others speculate on city spaces that are redefined and questioned by the deployment of what he calls 'vectors'. They resonate with the other great set of speculative spatial drawings: 'Chamber Works' by Daniel Libeskind. Both are charts of architectural possibility in a sea of technological and poetic uncertainty. Woods is a prime example of a speculative architect – always questioning and inventing.

Bioluminescence and Nanoluminescence

Electricity's reliance on coal-fired power stations and other limited mineral and petroleum resources makes finding an alternative energy source for lighting buildings' interiors and our external spaces one of the greatest challenges of the 21st century. Ken Yeang finds some clues for its resolution in existing biological and evolving artificial systems.

Can we produce light without electricity? Can we illuminate the interiors of our buildings and our cities at night without using electricity generated from renewable or non-renewable sources? Two systems are discussed here: the biological and the artificial.

The biological model involves learning from nature, reinventing from natural systems to benefit our human communities. The natural model is bioluminescence found in living organisms, which is the production and emission of light by an organism caused by a chemical reaction within or outside its cells, during which chemical energy is converted into light energy.

All living cells produce some degree of bioluminescence within the electromagnetic spectrum, each unique in wavelength, duration, timing and regularity of light flashes. However, this bioluminescence is visible to the naked eye only in certain species such as terrestrial organisms (fireflies,

certain centipedes and mushrooms), fish (for example, the cookie-cutter shark, marine hatchetfish, certain crustaceans, molluscs, clams and octopuses) and micro-organisms where it is used for camouflage, attraction, repulsion, communication and illumination.

In fireflies, bioluminescence is caused by the oxidation (the combination of a substance with oxygen) of the organic compound luciferin in the presence of the enzyme luciferase. Light flashes occur when the oxidating chemicals reach a high-energy state and then revert to their normal state. The rate of flashing is controlled by the firefly's nervous system and takes place in special air-tube-containing cells called photocytes.

A significant and beneficial difference between nature's way of generating light and that produced from electricity is that bioluminescent light, for example in fireflies, is heat-less. This chemically controlled 'cold light' contains no ultraviolet or infrared rays, and is emitted from the fly's lower abdomen. Yellow, green or pale red in colour, it has a wavelength of from 510 to 670 nanometers. More than 2,000 species of firefly can be found in

Macrophotograph of a firefly (family Lampyridae) in flight. This small beetle is named for its ability to flash its abdomen, as seen here. The production of light by an organism is known as bioluminescence. The firefly does this by using an enzyme (luciferase) to oxidise a chemical in a chamber in its abdomen. It controls the flashes by regulating the amount of oxygen that enters the chamber. The flashes of light are used to attract mates.

Underside of the firefly showing its
light organ at the tip of the abdomen.

temperate and tropical environments around the world, many in marshes or in wet, wooded areas where their larvae have abundant sources of food. The larvae can also emit light and are often called glow-worms. Scientists are currently studying these natural precepts to develop light source technologies that may one day become commercially viable.

In contrast to this natural production of light is its artificial descendant, nanoluminescence. Scientists are now developing a bio-friendly, electrode-free nano-sized light source capable of emitting coherent light across the visible spectrum. This nanowire light source is like a tiny flashlight that we can potentially scan across a living cell, visualising the cell while mechanically interacting with it. Production involves the creation of nanowires of potassium niobate synthesised in a special hot-water solution and separated using ultrasound. The wires produced are generally uniform in size, several microns long but only about 50 nanometers in diameter.

Nanoluminescence uses an infrared laser beam, and is thus still dependent on an external electrical energy source, to create an optical trap that allows the individual nanowires to be grabbed and manipulated. This same beam of infrared laser light also serves as an optical pump, causing the potassium niobate's unique non-linear optical properties to emit visible light in a range of different colours. The non-linear properties enable the frequencies of the incoming infrared light to be mixed or doubled, through techniques known respectively as second harmonic generation (SHG) or sum frequency generation (SFG), before being emitted as visible light. The light that is produced is tunable as well as coherent.

The nanowire light sources are then used to generate fluorescent light from specially treated beads as a spherical armature. Thus a nanowire in the grip of an infrared beam and in contact with a fluorescent bead causes the bead to become fluorescent with an orange colour at the point of contact.

As with bioluminescence, nanoluminescent light sources require further development before commercial production can become a real possibility. However, could the application of bioluminescence in our buildings one day provide light sources that imitate the production of light in nature, and the potential for illuminating our internal and external spaces with electricity- and heat-less light, thus reducing the carbon emissions from our built environment? Ð+

Ken Yeang is a director of Llewelyn Davies Yeang in London and TR Hamzah & Yeang, its sister company, in Kuala Lumpur, Malaysia. He is the author of many articles and books on sustainable design, including *Ecodesign: A Manual for Ecological Design* (Wiley-Academy, 2006).

MᶜLEAN'S NUGGETS

Float My Boat

Making slow progress down a Cumbrian street of two-storey terraces is the end section of *Ambush*, an Astute Class submarine. One of nine sections, this slow-moving cargo of 235 tonnes (259 tons) is moving at 4 kilometres (2.5 miles) an hour on a 48-wheeled Schelierle transporter, considerably slower than its eventual waterborne operating speed of 30 knots (55.5 kilometres/34.5 miles an hour).

Meanwhile, a report in *The Times* announces the recent launch of the world's largest passenger ship, the *Oasis of the Seas*, from Finnish shipbuilders STX Europe, weighing in at 130,218 gross tonnage (220,000 gross registered tonnage – GRT).[1] At 360 metres (1,181 feet) in length the ship is 50 metres (164 feet) longer than Renzo Piano's proposed London Bridge Glass Shard Building is in height, and features such *amuse-bouche* as the rising-tide bar – a kind of multilevelled deployable beverage offering. This vast cruise ship, brought to you by Royal Caribbean International, is so large that they have introduced the 'unique neighbourhood concept' which 'will provide guests with the opportunity to seek out relevant experiences based on their personal style, preferences or mood'[2] While these floating villages are always numerically impressive, stuffed full with enough luxury foodstuffs to fill innumerable kidney-shaped swimming pools, their trade appears to be to ply a very moribund brand of retroglamour and lumpen naval architecture (or was that navel?). Where are the new floating worlds of eco-civility, slowly circumnavigating, but not destroying (and even cleansing) the more aqueous regions of spaceship earth? Incidentally, the *Oasis of the Seas*, based on its passenger and crew's combined number of approximately 7,000, could berth 2.5 square kilometres (1 square mile) of a densely populated Singapore and 75 square kilometres (29 square miles) of the UK's less busy shores.[3]

In the grey-painted floating war zone of military hardware the argument for or against the Royal Navy's newly commissioned (and newly delayed) aircraft carriers should be had: weaponry or livingry anyone? Surely the offshore building capabilities of an island economy must be worth not only retaining but also developing and, more importantly, redeploying. Will Alsop's Hafen Pose Platz project for Bremen (*c* 1985) proposed a series of initiatives as a catalyst for the city's old docks, which included reactivating the 'skills and equipment of AG Weser (shipbuilders) to make buildings'.[4] This proposal seemed ideally suited for his practice's then elegant extrusions, which were as highly developed in cross section as any good ship. With Belfast's Harland and Wolff shipyard's recent diversification into offshore wind-power installation manufacture, why not more of this socially beneficial repurposing of industry? If the British government can commission two 66,000-tonne (65,000-ton) *Queen Elizabeth* class aircraft carriers, each to be made in four pieces at four different UK shipyards, why not extend the programme for such projects beyond military wherewithal?

The *Ambush* forward-end construction being moved to the Devonshire Dock Hall, Barrow-in-Furness, Cumbria.

Unmanageable

Martin Parker, writing recently in the *Observer* newspaper, asked the rhetorical question what do business and management schools actually teach? His answer: capitalism. He is highly critical of the narrow-focused conception of what this burgeoning university sector actually teaches, and states more precisely: 'If history departments teach about the past, and medical schools about the human body, then business schools should teach about organisations.'[5] This would probably include communes, co-ops, microcredit, localism, mutualism, anarchism, environmentalism, etc. Parker goes on to usefully suggest renaming these educational establishments 'Schools for Organising'.

Interesting 'management' models include that of Scott Bader Commonwealth, 'A British collaborative management-worker organisation designed to reduce industrial conflict and enhance working life for all.'[6] This international polymer and resins company was established by Ernest Bader in the 1920s. Bader was a pacifist and 'believed that business should serve society and that social conflict could be resolved through common ownership of industry'.

Interestingly, Dr EF Schumacher (author of *Small is Beautiful* (1973) and founder of the Intermediate Technology Development Group) served as a company director for Scott Bader. Other companies that eschew the top-down management model are WL Gore, makers of Gore-Tex and products ranging from guitar strings to the architectural fabric (fibre) Tenara®. CEO Terri Kelly is one of the company's few associates (there are approximately 8,000 worldwide) who has a job title, and while the company does have a structure with specialist divisions and business 'units', there is no hierarchy and hence no boss – a somewhat self-regulating business WL Gore is consistently voted one of the best companies to work for (or is that with?).[7] Another example is the highly successful Sheffield-based Swann Morton (www.swann-morton.com), best known for its surgical scalpel knives and blades (also very useful in the fabrication of architectural models). Swann Morton retains a unique ownership system whereby 50 per cent of the company is owned by the employees and 50 per cent by a charitable trust. Architectural practices unfortunately offer very few interesting models of enlightened employment, with the free (slave?) labour model of the celebrity practice internship particularly objectionable. △+

'McLean's Nuggets' is an ongoing technical series inspired by Will McLean and Samantha Hardingham's enthusiasm for back issues of AD, as explicitly explored in Hardingham's AD issue *The 1970s is Here and Now* (March/April 2005).

Will McLean is joint coordinator of technical studies (with Pete Silver) in the Department of Architecture at the University of Westminster. He recently co-authored, also with Pete Silver, the book *Introduction to Architectural Technology* (Laurence King, 2008).

Notes

1. 'Giant Liner Afloat for the First Time', *The Times*, 22 November 2008, p 16.
2. www.oasisoftheseas.com.
3. The population density figures are from the Economic and Social Research Council (ESCR) website: http://www.esrcsocietytoday.ac.uk/ESRCInfoCentre/facts/.
4. *Bridge/Beam/Floor/Roof: Projects concerning the use of the city and non-city as stimulated by carefully placed objects*, Catalogue to accompany an exhibition at the world's first out-of-town architecture centre, The Harbour, Bremen, May 1987.
5. Martin Parker, 'If Only Business Schools Wouldn't Teach Business', *Observer, Business*, 30 November 2008, p 8.
6. Richard CS Trahair, *From Aristotelian to Reagonomics: A Dictionary of Eponyms with Biographies in the Social Sciences*, Greenwood Publishing Group (Oxford), 1994, pp 569–70.
7. Simon Caulkin, 'Gore-Tex gets Made Without Managers', *Observer, Business*, 2 November 2008, p 9.

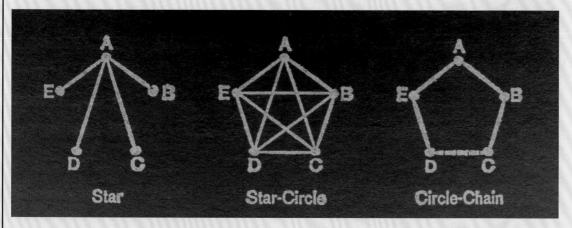

Three organisation networks. From Harold J Leavitt, *Managerial Psychology*, University of Chicago Press (Chicago, IL), 1964.

An Unconventional Low-Cost Museum

Valentina Croci describes how a diminutive museum dedicated to the feminine arts in Salerno, southern Italy, provides an intimate experience for visitors: its modest interior being enriched by an interface of information panels and interactive installations designed by Id-Lab in Milan.

ARC studio, Ghigos Ideas and Id-Lab Mirti, Museum for Feminine Arts (MAF), Vallo della Lucania, Salerno, Italy, 2008.
Museum curatorial project by Id-Lab and Nunzia Di Giacomo
The second floor deals with the theme of the Codes of Language or, more specifically, the meaning of recurring signs and ornamental motifs on fabrics. The display cases are constructed using the Stolmen system produced by IKEA. Particularly precious objects are located in Plexiglas containers, while others are suspended and can be touched. The display panels are important not only for the explanations of the collection that they provide, but also in smoothing out the appearance of the unfinished wall surfaces.

The MAF (Museo delle Arti Femminili/Museum of Feminine Arts) opened in October 2008 in Vallo della Lucania, a small town in the province of Salerno's mountainous Cilento peninsula, near the archaeological site of Paestum. The museum was created by a craft collector who, over decades, has gathered together arts and crafts pieces including lacework, embroidery, knitting and weaving, along with examples of the tools associated with such activities. The collection spans 300 years; however, it is not restricted to the area's local traditions and is better described as a testimonial to the many centuries-old skills and techniques that are now slowly disappearing.

Visitors to the museum are offered an exclusive vision of both the world of the collector and the little-explored reality of the feminine arts. The objects are displayed in a manner that seeks to highlight their network of meanings: their use, symbolism, and economic and cultural value. They are not classified by typology, but rather based on different themes: Memory, the Codes of Language, Patterns, Trades and Materials. Each theme has its own

floor of the building, which also contains workshops for further learning. More than a traditional museum, the structure is closer to a 'house-museum': a small space that can host only 10 visitors at a time. A guide conducts the visits, during which the public can interact with and touch the objects on display or try their hand in the workshops using various tools and techniques. The interior of the museum is an intimate space, thus each visit varies depending on the interests of the group and the dialogue created with the guide.

The MAF was designed by Milan offices Ghigos Ideas (Davide Crippa, Barbara Di Prete and Francesco Tosi) and Id-Lab (Line Ulrika Christiansen, Federico Esposito and Stefano Mirti) in collaboration with the local ARC Studio run by Gerardo del Gaudio. A low-cost museum, it uses only modified IKEA furniture, which was possible as the safety regulations of the 'house-museum' were less restrictive than those of a larger public museum. Also taking into account the small budget, the architectural finishes have been left in their rough state, exposing the various building systems. The mainly simple design is the result of much of the design work taking place off site in Milan, where the architects identified various solutions with ample margins for error that could be easily managed on site by local suppliers and professionals.

The Memory floor features a sound installation that is activated by visitors via a pressure sensor. Here they are told stories about the local area, and can listen to Cilento music and the sounds of tools at work, such as the hammering of a frame or a wool-winder turning.

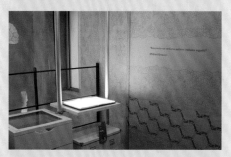

The third floor is dedicated to Pattern and features rare books that visitors can access via an interactive installation by Id-Lab. Using RFID sensor technology, a paper bookmark is placed on the blank page of a book to activate a video projection of the contents of the volumes on display. The texts and images for the exhibition are by Walter Aprile, Nunzio, Rosaria, Fortunata and Nunzia Di Giacomo.

The centre of the five-storey structure has been carved out to create an 18-metre (59-foot) tall courtyard that offers views of the various floors and access to the stairwell and elevator. From the third level upwards, the museum layout also includes areas dedicated to applied workshops.

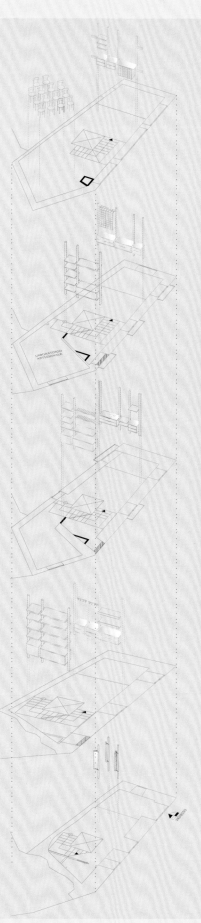

The architects have maintained the original facade. Only the windows have been treated with coloured films that correspond to the different themes on each floor of the museum. At night the facade becomes a sort of lighthouse, drawing attention to its presence and giving an unusual quality to the old town square.

On the level dedicated to Trades and the instruments of work is another interactive installation by Id-Lab. Using RFID technology, the visitor places a sensor over the area indicated on the panel to activate a video about the functioning of various tools. The adjacent room is dedicated to workshops.

The building, a five-storey tower owned by the family of the craft collector, is located in Vallo della Lucania's historic central square. Though it is of no particular historical value itself, the museum's location means that it is subject to restrictions imposed by the municipal government. The architects were therefore forced to leave the facade as it was, treating only the windows with different-coloured films that correspond to the content on each of the museum floors (the same colours are continued throughout the interiors) and at the same time set the building apart from its neighbours. At night the whole is transformed into an urban lighthouse, signalling its presence and giving an unusual quality to the old town square.

The floors of the tower are very narrow, measuring just 5 x 15 metres (16.4 x 49.2 feet). At the centre of the volume, a full-height inner courtyard has been created that allows access to the stairwell and elevator, and organises the overall taxonomy. The graphics and information panels hung on the walls of each floor, together with Id-Lab's interactive installations and the simple and intuitive layout are the museum's strongest points. As well as being instrumental to the visit and to learning about the collection, the information panels (covering a significant 30 square metres/323 square feet) at the same time serve to smooth out the surface of the unfinished walls.

The first floor deals with the theme of Memory, with historical photographs of the local population and an interactive acoustic installation in which three totems containing MP3 players activated by a pressure sensor offer visitors fragments of traditional Cilento music and the sounds of traditional tools being used in the domestic environments in which such activities once took place. The second floor covers the Codes of Language, demonstrating the meaning beyond the recurrent symbols

on lacework and embroidery. The third level presents the theme of Pattern: the recurring motifs or decorative intertwinings that make complex designs possible. Here visitors can flip through the contents of rare books presented in display cases in a video installation that uses RFID sensor technology. In a similar manner, on the fourth (Trades) floor, they are presented with images of the various tools of the trade as they were used. On the top floor visitors can see and touch natural materials: wool, silk, cotton, linen and hemp. The workshop in the adjacent space on this floor offers the possibility of experimenting with various techniques such as dyeing fabric and cotton- or wool-weaving.

The MAF works with local professional and educational institutions, actively promoting didactic activities for schools via organised visits and applied workshops. The world of the feminine arts thus becomes one of play for small children, or one of study and research for professionals (such as those from the nearby technical school of fashion). What is more, an intelligent management policy shared with private investors and public institutions helps attract regional tourism, taking advantage of the nearby archaeological site in Paestum. The theme of this house-museum, where the history of the collectors themselves is interwoven with the arts and crafts typical of the local area and traditional skills and techniques from further afield that are now disappearing, represents an instrument of economic growth tied to local and historical culture. MAF thus demonstrates how eccentricity – architectural, geographical and that of the collection itself – can become a strong point for developing cultural tourism and policy. Δ+

Translated from the Italian version into English by Paul David Blackmore.

Valentina Croci is a freelance journalist of industrial design and architecture. She graduated from Venice University of Architecture (IUAV), and attained an MSc in architectural history from the Bartlett School of Architecture, London. She achieved a PhD in industrial design sciences at the IUAV with a theoretical thesis on wearable digital technologies.

Tower Houses of Sana'a

Eric Firley, the co-author of a new compendium *The Urban Housing Handbook*, which investigates 30 major housing types from around the world, describes one of the most intriguing examples, situated in the Yemen on the Arabian Peninsula.

View from the terrace of a tall house over the roofs of the city and the neighbouring mountains.

For a Western observer, the tower houses of Sana'a in the Yemen probably represent one of the world's most unusual housing types. Having a minimal footprint but a high density overall, these beautiful family dwellings appear to grow out of the desert.

Sana'a's origins date back to the time of the reign of Saba (from approximately 1000 BC), when the Yemen (also called Arabia Felix) was a wealthy and important trade and garrison point on the ancient Incense Road. After a short Christian–Ethiopian period, in AD 628 Sana'a became Islamic and, due to its beautiful setting at an altitude of 2,500 metres (8,202 feet), its pleasant climate and its proud historical background, a major religious and educational centre of Islam. During the 17th and 18th centuries the city's trade monopoly in coffee brought it cosiderable wealth. Politically and architecturally, two Turkish occupations (1538–1629 and 1872–1918) had a long-lasting impact on the city's physical shape and the expressive decoration of its architecture.

The metropolitan area of Sana'a was limited to its walled Old Town until destruction of the wall in 1962. The following economic boom led to massive urban sprawl and the total inversion of the applied architectural type, which changed from the tower house to the Western villa, which

was built in the ever-growing suburbs. Today, the Old Town covers only 5 per cent of the total city area and its population has grown from about 80,000 to around 2 million.

Despite a very different kind of architecture and the absence of courtyard houses, the Old Town of Sana'a shares several urban similarities with other Islamic cities, notably the central position of the souks and the Friday Mosque as well as the grain and hierarchy of the urban layout. This generalisation should, however, not be taken too far, as the city structure indeed features several particularities, the existence of at least three distinct sectors – Arabic, Turkish and the former Jewish ghetto – being probably the most important. Each of the three sectors has been developed with other architectural types, and only the eastern Arabic area contains the here-depicted tower houses. All major quarters of the Arabic Old Town have their own mosque, hall and *hammam* (public bath), and are structured around a communal square known as the *Sarha*. Another morphological feature of crucial importance is the large fruit and vegetable gardens that help the dense urban structure breathe.

The internal organisation of the tower houses is based on a vertical subdivision around a central staircase. The ground and first floors are rather dark and simple: they are used as stables and storage areas for food, timber and other materials. Depending on the size of the house, the actual living areas develop from the third floor, sometimes even reaching eight storeys in height. As well as the private rooms, if there is enough space the third and fourth floors also have a reception and business room for guests and a diwan – a room reserved for special occasions and family celebrations. The top level of the house is usually set aside for the male residents and their guests, providing a magnificent view of the city. Directly linked to this covered space of Ottoman inspiration, known as the *mafraj*, are generous open terraces. The kitchen is underneath the top floor, facilitating the service in both directions – up to the top floor or down for predominantly family use.

The openings of the lower floors are very narrow, and gradually widen on the upper floors. In old buildings, before the use of glass, these were made with local alabaster. Today, most of them are colourful stained-glass windows that project a vibrant light onto the white internal walls, and do not allow direct views from the interior to the outside or vice versa.

The most impressive architectural feature of the tower houses is obviously their height. This is due to a lack of space in the walled town as well as to the need to save arable land, but it is also related to the city's historical vulnerability to enemy attack. As the political and geographical situation was unstable, the lower parts of the houses were designed to respond to a potential exterior threat. Ground floors were not therefore used as living areas, and the next level usually served as a generous storage area. However, these points alone do not stringently explain the genesis of an architectural type, and it seems that the real reason for the buildings' heights is a mixture of building tradition, wealth and architectural pride: as though the residents of Sana'a decided to compete with each other, and to invest a large proportion of their riches in the construction and gradual elevation of magnificent houses. 𝝙+

Eric Firley is an architect and urban designer. After studies in Lausanne, Weimar and London, he worked in several private practices and consulting companies in France and the UK. *The Urban Housing Handbook* is a project that he initiated in late 2005, and for which he and his co-author Caroline Stahl spent over two years on research and travels around the world. He is currently based in Paris.

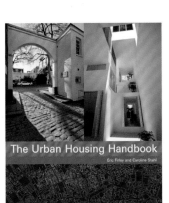

The Urban Housing Handbook by Eric Firley and Caroline Stahl, ISBN 978-0-470-51275-3, is published by John Wiley and Sons.

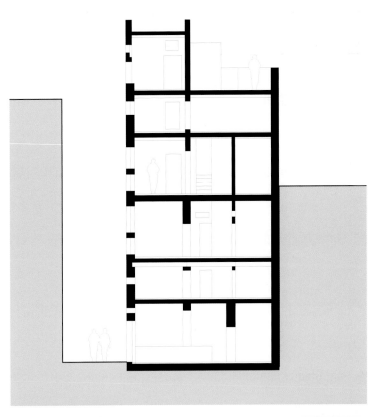

above: A typical streetscape with attached tower houses.
top: Section of a medium-sized house with six levels. Only the upper floors are used for living.

Architectural Design **Closing the Gap** March/April 2009

What is Architectural Design?

Launched in 1930, *Architectural Design* is an influential and prestigious architectural publication. With an almost unrivalled reputation worldwide, it is consistently at the forefront of cultural thought and design.

Architectural Design is published bimonthly. Features include:

Main section
The main section of every issue functions as a book and is guest-edited by a leading international expert in the field.

Δ+
The Δ+ magazine section at the back of every issue includes ongoing series and regular columns.

Truly international in terms of the subjects covered and its contributors, *Architectural Design*:

- focuses on cutting-edge design
- combines the currency and topicality of a newsstand journal with the rigour and production qualities of a book
- is provocative and inspirational, inspiring theoretical, creative and technological advances
- questions the outcomes of technical innovations as well as the far-reaching social, cultural and environmental challenges that present themselves today

How to Subscribe

With 6 issues a year, you can subscribe to Δ (either print or online), or buy titles individually.

Subscribe today to receive 6 issues delivered direct to your door!

£198 / US$369	institutional subscription (combined print and online)
£180 / US$335	institutional subscription (print or online)
£110 / US$170	personal rate subscription (print only)
£70 / US$110	student rate subscription (print only)

To subscribe: Tel: +44 (0) 843 828
Email: cs-journals@wiley.com

To purchase individual titles go to:
www.wiley.com